Dear John

I hope you enjoy
the read.
With warmest wishes

John M[?]ny

September 2015.

CANBERRA MMXV
Published by Halstead Press
Gorman House, Ainslie Avenue
Braddon, Australian Capital Territory, 2612
and
Unit 66, 89–97 Jones Street
Ultimo, New South Wales, 2007

ISBN 978 1 925043 12 9

CONTENTS

FOREWORD
"WHAT COULD POSSIBLY GO WRONG?"

John Mackay's antecedents and upbringing are not that unusual for the baby-boomer generation. It's much harder to understand why and how he came to enjoy such success in his exploits and what sets him apart. That's a central question you might keep in mind as you explore this book.

The book could easily have been titled What Could Possibly Go Wrong?. That familiar aphorism is often uttered by John about his next proposed venture, however outlandish.

John's distinguishing quality has been ability to harness an adventurous, resourceful, risk taking, even larrikin spirit to the disciplined requirements of a senior public servant and business leader. That's why he stands out among the talented people administering the nation's affairs. John also excels in his unflagging concern for others' welfare, whether employees where he works or community organisations seeking support. These are characteristics that have made him one of the outstanding misfits ever to rise to great heights in Canberra.

John's distinctive personality, achievements and generous community spirit make his story an absorbing and enjoyable read.

I first met John almost 40 years ago in a vain attempt to recruit him to my section of the Public Service Board. We've been mates ever since. I was privileged to speak at his 60th birthday and again in 2013 at his farewell as chairman of ACTEW and ActewAGL. It's no small honour then, to write this foreword.

For those wondering about my qualifications to do so, my upbringing and career paralleled John's in many ways. I went on to positions such as chief of staff to Prime Minister Keating and secretary of departments including Veterans Affairs, Transport and Development, and Defence. I completed my service to Australia's national interests as High Commissioner to New Zealand, retiring from that role to become Chancellor of the Australian National University. My work involves directorships on public and private sector boards including charitable and sporting organisations, and writing.

Some idea of John Mackay's measure can be found in his recent positions, chairing companies and government organisations, and directing important charities. He was made a Member of the Order of Australia in June 2004 and was appointed to the Chilean Bernardo O'Higgins Order in 2012.

John has used his influence wherever possible, on the rationale that a small amount of effort can make a very big difference to community causes. This sustained out of hours, personal effort is one of his admirable facets.

Born in Wellington, New South Wales, John finished school in 1968—an academic under-achiever whose purpose in life was to entertain the rest of the class. That larrikin trait lives on. Since he didn't qualify for university, John's father followed Mao Zedong's policy, sending him to work on a cotton farm to learn from the workers and contemplate his navel as a D8 bulldozer driver—a skill that has served him in good stead.

That led John to sit the public service entrance test and move to Canberra as a clerk where one day he encountered a pretty raffle ticket seller. John thought (rightly as it turned out) that he had won the raffle of his life when she later agreed to marry him and try valiantly to keep him grounded.

When he turned up at his future in-laws', Colette's father Rex didn't think that if John was a horse in the Inglis saleyard, trainer Tommy Smith would have paid top dollar for him. But John shone before long. He graduated as Bachelor of Administration and Economics with a final year prize as top student. His mother nearly fainted. John went on to be a tutor, guest lecturer, Council member and chancellor at his alma mater. His time at Canberra University proved to be life changing.

He next spent a considerable time climbing the public service ladder to the level of deputy secretary, with a stint as senior adviser to the Minister for Administrative Services. Then, as Head of the Australian Protective Service, John developed his penchant for dressing up and courting the media.

Cubs, Scouts and school cadets, adherence to the "Be Prepared" motto, and incurable optimism inherited from his mother—all served to hone his leadership skills.

John has never forgotten his roots and four lessons of life that underpin his remarkable contribution:

- —manage yourself with high levels of discipline
- —use the privilege and influence of your job to help the less fortunate
- —do your best to apply a positive attitude, and
- —rise early and work hard.

The only people who never made a mistake are those that weren't trying hard enough. How you deal with mistakes reveals your true character. Hypercritical Canberra commentators who revel in schadenfreude and lopping tall poppies are invaluable to that end.

There's more to come in the John Mackay story. I hope this little gem of a book will give you as much enjoyment as it has me, and a few lessons about how to live a good and meaningful life.

– Dr Allan Hawke, AC, FAIM, FAICD, FIPAA

INTRODUCTION
EARLY SIGNS OF THE
FIREWORKS TO COME

The nine year old boy lit a huge bunger and dexterously lobbed it into the back of a passing utility. Then came an explosion and the rapid return of the vehicle and its infuriated driver, not unreasonably concerned about the risk to the fuel he was transporting.

In so many ways it was just a normal day in the early life of John Angus Mackay, second of seven children growing up in the otherwise quiet town of Wellington, in the central west of New South Wales. A small boy for his age, but never intimidated by that. Not a boy attracted to schooling, but one who tried never to miss school—because he wanted to be with his mates.

Away from school, the great challenge was which form of entertainment to choose. Swimming, cycling, shooting, hunting and of course fireworks were among the options that ensured he was never bored. A lifelong love of cars began years before he held a driving licence. Undaunted by major crashes, he remained a risk taker and later retained an uncanny knack of surviving serious physical injury and averting major damage to his public service career.

Thanks to that career, most Canberra residents are familiar with the public persona of John Mackay. Few would know of his commitment to three wayward brothers. Two of them died from AIDS and one served ten years in prison. Nor would many know of the responsibility he accepted as the eldest son, but still a young child in his large family, when his father, out of work, drunk and depressed, threatened the family with violence.

This background has made a man who is optimistic, compassionate and a strong influence on the life of a city and the nation. A man who says with understatement, "I think I have lived a fair bit on the edge."

How he lived that way as he made major contributions at the top levels of government and business administration, and to charitable causes, is the subject of this book.

John Mackay, aged 11, on the family car, perhaps pondering his future direction, near Pallamallawa in north western New South Wales, 1961.

AUTHOR'S NOTE

Soon after I left full time employment, I lunched with John Mackay, primarily to fulfil a commitment of several years' standing. Still quite lost in my new world of retirement, I spoke of some hopes and fears for the future.

This included my continuing interest in recording oral history. He intimated there were aspects of his life he would like recorded. About six months later, the day after he announced his intention of resigning as chair of ACTEW Corporation and ActewAGL, I phoned to suggest we pursue the idea, and learnt that he had written some notes but was unsure of their value. A friend who had looked at them told him the effect was something like "The Sound of Music" with the sound turned off.

Feeling there was nothing to lose, I offered to read them myself. Within a few minutes of beginning, I phoned to ask if I could write his biography. If nothing else it would fill the void created by my retirement and there was at least the possibility that between us we would produce something for posterity.

So here is the result. Not a definitive account but primarily the result of six lengthy recorded interviews with John Mackay, one with his youngest daughter, Claire, and one with his wife, Colette, supplemented by research to clarify facts.

I had interviewed John Mackay on the day in 1999 when he was announced as the new head of ACTEW Corporation. From then on we spoke regularly as part of my role as a journalist, seeking explanations for failures and successes in the supply of water, electricity and gas to Canberra.

Generally I eschewed a bevy of public relations staff, finding it much faster and more enlightening to speak with the man himself. Through his frankness, honesty and good humour, and what I hope was my fair reporting of many matters, we developed a mutual trust.

We had little else in common, save that we were born in the same hospital, me first by about 18 months. Yet during the writing of this book, the frankness, honesty and good humour have remained. He has corrected factual errors but has not sought to have any detail excised that might promote adverse reflection on himself.

I thank John Mackay for the opportunity to write this book. I also thank John Carrick, of Sydney, for his initial editing and his enthusiasm.

My particular thanks go to Matthew Richardson, of Halstead Press, who on the strength of one telephone call agreed to consider the manuscript and within a few days to negotiate its publication. Thanks too are due to William Hall, of Living Portraiture, who took several of the photographs including the front cover and who brilliantly restored the old photographs used in this book.

GROWING UP SMART

John Mackay's father, Jackson Angus Mackay, was born in St Kilda in 1905. He died on 28 January 1980 from cirrhosis of the liver.

John's grandfather, William Angus Mackay, was born in Tumut in 1865 and died in Sydney in 1927. He was educated at Sydney Grammar School after which he became a stock and station agent in Deniliquin and later in Dubbo. John's great grandfather, Angus Mackay, came to Australia in about 1853 from the Isle of Skye in Scotland. He was wealthy when he arrived, or soon after, and owned Pommagalana station in the Wagga Wagga district.

William (Billy) married Maude Alice King and they settled in the Riverina, at one stage owning most of the land around Wagga Wagga. The well to do family, with polo ponies and a suite permanently booked in Melbourne's Windsor Hotel, could send Jackson (Jack) and his brother Reg to the best schools.

The family, like so many others in Australia, was hit hard by the Depression. For reasons unknown, they sold their Wagga land to the government. They invested the proceeds in a 10,000 acre wheat crop, which was ruined by a hailstorm shortly before harvest.

Jack, having already survived major surgery to remove part of a lung, headed for Dubbo to work as a stock and station agent. By then he had left behind his first wife and daughter. (Later, many years would pass before John Mackay made contact with his half sister who, coincidentally, had lived in Canberra for some years.)

Left to right: John's mother Betty (left), with her sisters Nancye and Margaret in 1945. The three sisters served in the Women's Air Force in World War II.

As part of his job in Dubbo, Jack travelled widely around western New South Wales. He met his second wife, Betty Digges, shortly before World War Two. They married in Coonamble on 11 January 1946.

Jack served in the War from 20 August 1941 to 13 February 1946. His preference had been to join the RAAF but, having failed a medical exam, he spent most of the War in an Army tank crew. He was stationed at Rabaul in New Guinea from 25 August 1944 to 6 January 1946.

His military record shows him as three years younger than his actual age. His height was recorded as 5 feet 6½ inches. The record also details his having an appendix scar, although it was in fact the huge scar from the lung surgery.

Jack's wife Betty and her two sisters, Margaret and Nancye, were educated at the Presbyterian Ladies' College in the inner western Sydney suburb of Croydon. During the war she and her sisters joined the Women's Air Force and were based in Townsville, Sydney and Melbourne, driving ambulances and staff cars.

Betty's parents, Thomas and Thelma Digges, were wealthy. They owned three cars before anyone else in Coonamble had one. However, it seems that the Depression, followed by World War Two, had reduced Thelma, the only grandparent John ever met, to living on the pension for all her later years.

Betty's father Thomas J. Digges, born in 1884, married Thelma Grace Cleaver, born in 1896, in Orange in 1916. Thomas Digges's grandfather, Thomas Blackstock Digges, was born in Ireland in 1826 and travelled to Australia on the ship *Herald*.

In 1856 Thomas Blackstock Digges married Christina Cameron in Mudgee and in 1861 their son Charles Henry Digges was born at Mendooran. He married Elizabeth Sullivan in 1880; in 1884, Betty's father (John Mackay's grandfather) was born.

Thomas's obituary said he had been a founding member of the Coonamble Bowling Club and, against stern opposition, had gained its first liquor licence. "Of a jovial nature, [he] was one of the most popular men in the district, always looking on the bright side of life, and many times he was able to bring a fellow man out of the depths of depression with his cheerful attitude."

Betty was born in Dubbo on 5 April 1918, and inherited her father's positive attitude.

After marriage, Betty and Jack lived for a short time in Kings Cross before moving to Wellington, a pretty town on the confluence of the Macquarie and Bell rivers, about 360 kilometres west of Sydney.

Wellington was a small but important rural centre for wheat and wool. It had about ten hotels and licensed clubs and four banks. There was a large Aboriginal population, most of whom lived at a mission; the remainder lived in corrugated iron shanties just out of town. There were market gardens owned by descendants of the Chinese from the mid-19th century gold rush. A more recent Greek population grew olives and owned cafes. Construction of Burrendong Dam in the late 1950s brought an influx of European migrants, among others.

Betty and Jack Mackay in 1947.

Wellington's population of about 4,600 has changed little since John Mackay left school there in 1968.

The area was originally home to the Wiradjuri people. Explorer John Oxley was the first European to visit the district, which he named Wellington Valley in 1817.

Oxley was impressed by the area's suitability for agriculture and a convict settlement was established close to the present town site in 1823. The site was abandoned about seven years later and in 1831 the few buildings erected by the convicts were given to the Church Missionary Society, which established a mission for the Aborigines.

The Society later objected to the establishment of a town, which it said would interfere with missionary work. However, the mission closed in the early 1840s and the town of Wellington was proclaimed in 1846.

The town continues to serve the surrounding rural district but has largely been supplanted in the wider region by the bigger cities of Dubbo, 50 kilometres from Wellington, and Orange, 100 kilometres away.

Jack Mackay, after settling in Wellington with his new wife, again worked as a stock and station agent. Their first child, Anne, was born in 1948. John Angus Mackay was born in August, 1950, followed by David, Philip, Mark, Stephen and Lizzie, and Anthony who died soon after birth.

The Mackay children in 1955, from left: Anne holding Mark, with John, David and Philip.

Dressed for success: from left, Philip, John and David at Wellington Primary School in 1958.

Jack was 42 when Anne was born, and Betty was 30. Jack was 55 and Betty 43 when Lizzie was born. Perhaps their age difference and advancing years meant that the family experience of each child varied markedly.

The family home was at 93 Maughan Street, Wellington. From this modest street also came a Qantas pilot and a professional golfer.

Life for the growing family had its share of challenges, not least the heavy drinking of both parents, particularly Jack. Despite this, John remembers both parents fondly and with obvious deep respect. There seems little doubt that his father's dark moods and occasional violence were largely the result of his war service in New Guinea where, like many others, he caught malaria.

Jack suffered from a condition that would now almost certainly be described as post-traumatic stress disorder. This occasionally caused the family to summon their doctor at midnight. John remembers the frustrated doctor telling Jack, "If you do not behave I will have you certified."

In a particularly disturbing episode when John was about 11, he and his mother locked themselves in a bedroom while his father beat at the door with an axe. At other times Jack would sing war songs or regale the family with unpleasant war stories. He remained bitter about the Japanese.

Despite his heavy drinking and occasional dark moods, Jack would rise early the day after such an episode. He was industrious and something of a raconteur.

Jack's job took him long distances; although he was regarded as a good driver, he smashed up many cars. He was a proud man and would almost never go anywhere without being well attired, complete with hat, and meticulously groomed.

Though his father's occasional outbursts were disturbing, John is philosophical about their long term effect on his life. "The recollection I have is that when you got to school the next morning you weren't Robinson Crusoe."

Many families had fathers who had been to the War. Young John Mackay did not believe his family was markedly different from many. Indeed, he said the good times significantly outweighed the bad.

Betty ran the house, but in contrast to a typical country woman, she was not a great cook. Perhaps because of this, and despite the family's being not particularly well off, there was nearly always a maid, even during family holidays.

John Mackay credits his mother with inculcating his incurable optimism. She was resourceful and a skilful manager, who enjoyed a drink and was a heavy smoker. By age 15 her eldest son was smoking regularly.

When the stock and station agency closed, there were five or six kids, no car and no job, in a small country town that offered few opportunities.

Young John might be sent to the shops to buy, on credit, cigarettes for his father and butter for the family. Successively, their credit at the shops dried up and John had to learn how to supplement the family's limited income.

There was a market then for old rags and a relatively reliable supply. There was also a market for lead, which John would remove from derelict houses and collect by digging spent bullets from the butts at the local rifle range. He used some of this money to buy food for himself instead of going home for lunch. But he was also skilled in cultivating friends whose mothers were good cooks.

These friends included Russell Rogers, whose parents owned a hotel where food was plentiful. For young John, the evolving larrikin, the venue had the added advantage of a balcony overlooking the street, from which he and Russell targeted with shanghais the tempting rear ends of passers-by.

Johnny Preston's mother was also a good cook. She would ask if John would like to stay for dinner, and he often did. This suited Betty's strategy of taking various opportunities to relocate one or other of her brood. She would arrange for a child to visit an aunt for a weekend or longer. Ingeniously, she would persuade the family GP, Dr Barton, to send a child to hospital with the most minor ailments.

Betty was a great delegator. Regardless of who you were, you would rarely be in her presence for very long without being given a task to perform, often in a subtle or indirect way. She would say something like, "I'll get on with that washing up after you leave."

John, who missed about a year of schooling with bronchitis, once spent almost a week in hospital with an infected finger. Obviously the pressure on hospitals then, at least in Wellington, was not as great as it is now.

In those days, particularly in the country, water for baths was often heated in a copper. When the copper failed, the washing machine provided hot water; when the washing machine also broke down, John's mother remained undaunted. She travelled to Dubbo and returned with a chip heater that she evidently could not afford. It was repossessed before the family could use it.

John recalled only one occasion when his mother had simply had enough, possibly at about the time his father had lost his job. Coming home that day, he asked his brothers where their mother was. She had gone to the railway station with her bag and he set out after her.

He met his mother at the railway station and convinced her to come home with him.

"I don't think that was an easy talk. But she didn't get on the train, thank God."

As they walked home together, John carried her bag.

At a particularly bad time his father was deeply depressed and took the garden hose and got into the car ready to drive away. John, well aware of the likely consequence, jumped in and went with his father, and brought him home. On other occasions John would sit with his father when he seemed to be hallucinating. "I guess that was a bit of a responsibility," he says.

Much later, when his father was old, money was scarce and good times were rare, his mother became an Avon lady, selling cosmetics door to door. She was a natural saleswoman and made enough money to fund several trips around Australia and overseas. Instead of being painfully isolated at home with no money, the job gave her enjoyable social contact for many years. She continued to sell cosmetics until she was 80 and drove her car for some years after that.

Even during times of privation, particularly after Jack Mackay lost his job, the family retained reasonable harmony. Life was frugal, with basic but nutritious food. John would prepare the family's breakfast of a large pot of porridge or rice.

As the eldest son, he took his family responsibility seriously. When aged about ten he painted the entire house. Not grudgingly but with considerable enthusiasm. He also made repairs to furniture and laid linoleum in the kitchen.

John also set to work on the family fruit trees, often having been asked by his father to help with pruning. His father, with both feet firmly on the ground, directed the operation, pointing out branches that needed lopping while John climbed the trees and did all the work. On his own initiative, he established vegetable gardens in the backyard.

There were other ways for a resourceful boy to make money. He bought day old chicks which he raised and sold. This venture was not entirely legal as he took most if not all of the food for the chickens from nearby wheat silos. The same handy food source sustained a later enterprise of raising homing pigeons. For other income he picked potatoes and marked lambs.

Some of the financial pressure was relieved when Jack started selling insurance. By then, John had established a lucrative business in trapping and selling rabbits, often referred to as "underground mutton".

An enjoyable outing for father and son was a day's fishing on the banks of the Macquarie River. They caught a 3kg and 2kg Murray cod and a 3kg yellow-belly (golden perch). They were on a bank a couple of metres above the water so they had to improvise with a second line to hook and land the fish. John also spent many days angling for catfish with his mates near the town's waterworks.

Then there were the guns. John and various mates had slug guns from about the age of ten. He graduated to a .22 rifle by age 12 or 13 and used it on frequent trips to Bakers Swamp, about 15km south of Wellington, shooting rabbits with Bruce (Bushy) Bell. There were rabbits in their thousands and the boys, with Bruce's father, an excellent bushman, would shoot, trap and sell their prey. A further advantage was that Bruce's mother was yet another fantastic cook.

From about the age of 12, John mainly supported himself. As a teenager, he spent about 20 weekends each year at the Bells' place. On a reasonable weekend he could make about half the basic wage (perhaps equal to some $300 at current value) from the sale of rabbits for about five shillings a pair. On a really good weekend they would sell about 30 rabbits.

John worked at a supermarket on Friday afternoons and Saturday mornings, packing groceries and lugging weights as heavy as 30kg bags of flour several hundred metres to the cars of female customers. After work on Saturdays he would hitchhike to Bruce Bell's to go rabbiting. Before catching the school bus on Monday mornings they would check the rabbit traps. He also ran a successful lawnmowing business and helped with fencing, potato picking and bean picking. He was less successful at the latter because his colour-blindness led to confusion between beans and weeds. Then there was the milk run, which began at 3 a.m. every Monday, Wednesday and Friday before school.

Even then, with much time spent away from home with friends, John retained considerable responsibility for the family. His elder sister Anne was a mentor for him, particularly as he began high school. John didn't know how to dance or even how to dress well for functions. So Anne lined up some female school friends, including a girl from down the road, Lindy Tainton, who taught John how to stomp, twist—and kiss.

Standard teenage male dress for social occasions was skin tight Amco jeans, black skivvies and desert boots. Later came Beatles outfits and pointy toed shoes.

John and Anne were more like each other than like their other siblings, three of whom would cause great heartache to the family through heroin addiction. John did not know it then, but two brothers were gay and would later die from AIDS.

David, gregarious and highly entertaining, was loved by everyone. A performance at a school review exemplified his ability to captivate an audience. Stephen was immature until the day he died; Mark, blessed with a high IQ, was constantly expelled from school and later spent ten years in prison. He continues to depend on John for the occasional handout. That he survived at all was extraordinary. Philip joined the Post Office, where he worked until his retirement; Lizzie, who became good friends with John, was still young when he left home.

There were some really likeable teachers in primary school and it was a social place to meet up with mates. John began school at four but was the last to learn the alphabet, after being stood in the corner until he learned it. "But I probably knew how to set a rabbit trap better than anybody else."

His sense of humour got him into trouble often. He would usually be the first to laugh, which of course distracted the rest of the class. During an Anzac Day ceremony, the Last Post, played through the school's poor quality speakers, sounded less than heart breaking and more like a fart. Of course John laughed, followed by the entire class and the teacher, a returned serviceman, gave him a flogging for inciting disruption.

This was neither the first nor the last such punishment. He once made a paper aeroplane and fitted an ink nib to the nose. A well aimed shot left the plane fixed to the ceiling and the class erupted in laughter. The entire class was threatened with a flogging until he confessed. As he climbed a ladder to reach the aircraft, he gleefully imagined it falling nib first onto the teacher's bald head.

Wellington Primary School had high roofs, which made recovery of tennis balls thrown by the students difficult. The headmaster agreed to John's offer to get the balls down. He was to get the ladder and wait until the headmaster came to supervise.

The ladder reached four or five metres from the ground but not quite up to the guttering. Well before the headmaster arrived John, strongly encouraged by the other students, had managed to scramble onto the roof and began firing tennis balls at his young audience below. Having recovered all of them he began the descent, clinging to the guttering while trying to regain the ladder with his feet. The guttering gave way. Boy and ladder fell to the ground, leaving John covered in mud and groaning, just as the headmaster arrived.

Fortunately, there were no injuries, and the headmaster was better disposed to him than the other teachers. The headmaster was a returned serviceman who knew Jack and Betty.

"He often flogged other kids I was with, gave me a lecture about what nice people my parents were and what a disgrace I was to them, then let me go."

Despite this discipline was frequent. In high school John was caned almost weekly, sometimes for offences as minor as saying something silly in class or for a misjudged prank.

Mostly the punishment was a cut across the hand which would sting for about 30 minutes but a couple of teachers—Redhead Smith and Nifty Croft in particular—gave canings that really hurt. Nifty applied the cane with such force that his feet would leave the ground.

Despite the pain these punishments were untroubling—more a badge of honour than anything to regret.

One great pleasure was to play up in an art class with several mates. When the teacher turned her back he would throw clay balls which stuck to the blackboard. The teacher could not tell who to blame, and the goody-two-shoes, having not been caned before, would have to share in the indiscriminate punishment.

The two final years of primary school brought dancing lessons each Friday. For sins young John committed elsewhere around the school, one teacher engineered the novel punishment of making him dance with the least attractive girl in the class. The chosen girl, knowing she had been selected as punishment, surely suffered because of this teacher's thoughtlessness.

Presumably his reputation did not precede him from primary school, because in his first year of high school John was given the incongruous responsibility of lighting heaters in all the classrooms. Contrary to the best safety practice of lighting the taper before turning on the gas, John soon learned that by counting to three between turning on the gas and lighting the taper, he could produce something like a sonic boom, much to the amusement of fellow students.

John had no real urge to read or learn: "For all the benefit John gets out of this class, he may as well not attend", said one of his school reports, and another—"John seems to think that the only reason for coming to school is to entertain the rest of the class."

In high school he was naturally good at mathematics, woodwork and metalwork. But he did not thrive in English, which he found boring, and his academic progress was limited. He was always challenging authority and frequently rebellious in the classroom, but school was not the only source of education.

2

THE BASICS: SCOUTING, SCAMMING, SMUGGLING

"I probably learned more from Scouts and Cadets than I ever did from the traditional classroom," John said.

He was introduced to Scouting as a Cub Scout at seven. His achievements there were recognised with many badges and he was given some leadership responsibility. In 1961, as a Cub Scout, he visited the Australian Scout Jamboree at Landsdowne in New South Wales. Away from the familiar Wellington community, he realised that there were people in the world beyond his home town, state and nation.

John describes himself as resourceful. He attributes this at least initially to Scouting, where he learned practical skills such as lighting fires under most conditions, reading maps and basic first aid. He remains confident that if stranded in the Brindabella ranges west of Canberra, he could keep himself alive, find his way out or help rescuers to locate him.

"None of my mates in those early days had much going for them. Neither did I. We were focussed on fun and adventure rather than school."

Yet despite the larrikin tendency he became a dedicated Scout, learning about survival and leadership. He spent a lot of time in the bush: hiking, camping, navigating, cooking and skylarking. Resourcefulness was a trait much valued by the founder of Scouting, Lord Robert Baden-Powell. But some of Scout John Mackay's resourcefulness might well have sent a tremor through the grave in Kenya where Baden-Powell was buried in January 1941.

In late December 1964 scouts going from Wellington to the seventh Australian Scout Jamboree in Dandenong, Victoria, caught a train to Sydney, where they boarded a dedicated, dilapidated train for the journey to Melbourne. Even by the standards of the day, this train was unsuitable for transporting hundreds of boys.

John Mackay was enthusiastically among those who spent much of the journey dangling their legs over the edge of the open platforms between the carriages. There was little to prevent anyone falling off, either to the side or between the carriages.

Everyone survived and John arrived safely at the Jamboree with the several cartons of cigarettes he would sell for a fair profit. The Jamboree extended into the second week of January. Not long after arriving, John pinched a book of pass-out tickets which he issued to himself and his mates. They spent about half the Jamboree at Melbourne's attractions, particularly Luna Park.

But he undertook all of his camp duties, including cooking, at which he was more than proficient. He was also continuing to appreciate that there was more to the world than Wellington, where people were not much concerned with major world or even national events. But tell them that a local they knew had just knocked over a guidepost and there would be considerable interest. The Jamboree, with Scouts from other countries, was quite an eye-opener.

Back in Wellington, Redhead Smith, the English teacher, was known to leave the school at morning break for the nearby bowling club where he would steady his nerves with a bracing couple of drinks. Clearly he was not popular with some of his students. A group of them passing his house on the way home from Scouts thought it a good idea to shout five or six times, "Redhead is a deadhead."

Soon after, as they made their way home, Redhead in his speeding Vauxhall nearly ran over the entire group. John, perhaps unwisely, loaned him a pencil to write down the names of the offenders.

A couple of days later, with considerable foreboding, John entered the English class. Smith announced to the class the nature of the lesson and wrote the relevant instructions on the blackboard. But to John he said, "I want you to write an essay on the Boy Scouts' motto—Be Prepared. And blimey son you'd better be!"

Smith caught up with each of the offending Scouts, using their most minor indiscretions for severe canings; one fainted under the onslaught.

Even as young Scouts, John and a few others would go with no adult supervision to a small hut in the bush for a weekend. They built things—flying foxes, chairs, tables and even a bed.

At his first cadet camp John Mackay, ever the opportunist, noticed that there was no sugar. So he took a great deal of sugar to the next camp and sold it at a considerable profit.

But despite his shenanigans, John in turn became top Cub Scout, top Scout and top cadet in Wellington. These organisations recognised qualities of leadership that contrasted with his natural, larrikin approach to life and mediocrity at school.

Betty Mackay encouraged her son's participation in Scouts and cadets, which he attributes to her managerial style of reducing the number of kids around the house. The other brothers were not involved in Scouting but all achieved minor ranks in the cadets.

John was good at bushcraft, tying knots and dealing with almost any situation. Later on, his wife believed him capable of managing all emergencies. He attributed this largely to the lessons of life from Scouts and cadets, whereas formal education was simply a means to an end and not something he particularly wanted.

In his job as a stock and station agent Jack Mackay travelled extensively around the west of New South Wales, often accompanied by his eldest son. That suited his wife, with her aim to get people out of the house.

Almost at the beginning of Australia's live sheep trade, Jack spent many weeks in his job buying sheep for export to Chile. He arranged transport for the sheep to Sydney and took John with him to see them loaded onto the ship *Delfino*.

An associate of Jack's, Gordon Forsyth, was on the ship, sporting a beautiful pair of knee high cowboy boots from South America. Young John coveted those boots and took seriously a suggestion by Forsyth that he travel on the ship to South America. It was never going to happen, but John would have loved to travel on that ship to wangle a pair of those impressive cowboy boots.

On a visit to Manilla in the early 1990s he eventually did get a colourful pair. He still occasionally wears classic R.M. Williams knee high boots.

Soon after he lost his job, Jack worked for a short time managing a wheat stack at Biniguy near Moree. John stayed there with him for about six weeks over the summer school holidays. They lived in a shed at Pallamallawa and shared a single bed and a hurricane lamp on a packing case .

While his father worked all day, John played in the wheat stack, shot pigeons or spent time with newfound mates and railway fettlers. He enjoyed these trips away with his father.

In those days in rural areas, it was common enough for parents to teach children how to drive while they were quite young, and John was probably about 11 when he learnt. Like his father, he drove fast and racked up numerous crashes. He admits to being fortunate not to have been killed several times. Driving lessons for all the Mackay kids took place on the town common. By about 14 John was a competent driver, or might have been if he had applied less pressure to the accelerator.

Betty's and Jack's propensity to get on the grog most nights provided ample opportunities to purloin the car keys and take the car without them knowing. Making use of a slope John could push the car out of the drive and down the road before starting the motor. He would pick up some mates and go for a drive, sometimes to Dubbo, about 50 kilometres away. "One of my mates decided to run away from home so I dropped him in Orange."

That would have been a round trip of about 200 kilometres.

When about 14 years old, he drove the family car at 160 km/h. Once he was caught by a neighbour as he was pushing the car out. Another time, Jack woke and hearing rain, remembered that he had left the car windows open. But the car wasn't there and he quickly guessed who had it.

Living on the edge, an 11 year old John Mackay rides on a truck loaded with grain at Biniguy near Moree in north-western New South Wales in 1961.

Even before John had a driver's licence, about three months before turning 17, he bought his first car, a 1957 VW Beetle, in a joint venture with Betty. It expanded her freedom of movement when Jack was out of town with the family car.

It also increased John's freedom. One Saturday morning, his parents were in the main street when John drove past in the VW, with his L-plates displayed but no licensed driver in the car, as the law required.

After about 18 months, the VW was replaced by an FB Holden. The almost obligatory exhaust extractors and twin carburettors were soon added, increasing the noise, speed and fuel consumption.

John Mackay says Wellington was like many rural centres that

The start of a lifelong affair with wheeled vehicles: John (third from front) and friends on a three seater bike in 1965. His lifelong mate Johnny Preston is at the front.

bred kids to leave. But the town provided his generation with considerable freedom. There was no lack of entertainment: you could swim and canoe in the river when not involved in rabbiting or one of the many other pursuits on offer.

He was surrounded by good mates, including one of Aboriginal descent, one of Chinese descent, and another who was the son of German immigrants recently arrived, in town to work on the dam. John was blissfully unaware of racism. But as in many other western New South Wales towns, Aboriginal people were generally regarded as the lower class and treated accordingly. He recalls residents of two Aboriginal missions being always in trouble.

One of his mates, Terry Ogg, who lived around the corner, invited John several times to go smuggling. Unaware of what this might entail, but having some idea it would involve them getting up to no good, John waited awake for Terry over several nights, then concluded he wasn't coming.

John was asleep in the bedroom he shared with three brothers when Terry eventually tapped on their window, which had been broken by a stray stone or ball, and whispered that it was time to go. This startled John's brother David who screamed that a burglar was at the window.

Their father armed himself with a souvenir Samurai sword he had obtained in New Guinea, and raced into the yard. He thrust the sword into shrubs and trees around the house, including the one occupied by the would-be smuggler in the foetal position. The cold steel must have gone close to the fugitive.

Waiting for the school bus next morning, Terry told John, "Your old man nearly stabbed me."

And so ended their careers as smugglers.

Jack Mackay rarely attended church—a few weddings and his funeral, as John recalls it. Betty, who was a regular churchgoer until her death, insisted on her son attending the Presbyterian Sunday School. But John remains largely agnostic about the existence of God. Like much of his schooling, he regarded Sunday School as a social outing. "And I had plenty of other social outlets where you didn't have to learn catechism."

Later in life he would work with numerous religious-based organisations. They had him saying prayers, sometimes three times in a week. Over a 15 year period he chaired a Salvation Army advisory board, was a director of Little Company of Mary Healthcare and worked with the Anglican Church on a land redevelopment. "I have always thought, just in case there is somebody up there, I had better take out some insurance."

God as explained in Sunday School seemed about as real as Santa Claus. "But I haven't still ruled out converting to become a Catholic." If he did, it would be as a support to his wife, a practising Catholic.

A GOOD GROUNDING IN EXPLOSIVES

When a child goes missing, especially in a country town, the community is bound to be involved in the search. So it was when Philip Mackay, John's eight year old brother, ran away from home, apparently after eating more than his share of something his mother had left on the kitchen table. Either expecting or being threatened with a thrashing, he decamped.

A characteristic of the Mackay parents' administration of discipline was that punishment could not be saved for later. So the kids understood that if they could delay punishment, particularly physical punishment, it would normally not occur. If Philip could make himself scarce for a while, he was unlikely to be punished. Perhaps he had learned this from John, who had demonstrated that if he escaped before being caught around the legs by the ironing cord, it would not be applied later.

Philip had not been found when darkness fell. His concerned parents involved neighbours in the search. Then the entire town was notified by a radio broadcast. So began a major search including the rivers and park.

One of the searchers went into the house to check on the other two younger brothers, who were sharing a double bed. The searcher tripped in the cluttered bedroom and found Philip asleep under the blankets.

At high school, John had a great mate, Johnny (Prep) Preston, who lived in a shed behind his mother's house and was effectively free to do as he pleased. They used the freedom of Johnny's accommodation to build things with their other great mate, Paul (Louie) Lousick.

Their creations included crystal sets and even a three seater bicycle. They built a wooden suitcase into which was fitted a winder from an old telephone. The current produced from this contraption was sufficient to deliver a significant electrical shock to an unsuspecting character more than 20 metres away.

They also made crossbows, skateboards, shanghais and gun silencers as well as producing gunpowder and hydrogen from caustic soda and aluminium milk bottle tops.

John and Prep both had homing pigeons and thought nothing of going at night to the silo by the railway to get wheat to feed their birds. In similar spirit they ventured at night to the high railway bridge where they caught pigeons.

As it happened, on the other side of the railway bridge was a Girl Guide camp. So the boys, aged about 15, paid a courtesy visit, after lights out when the girls were in bed. It was "all pretty bloody innocent, but in other ways probably not so innocent," John recalls.

Prep, who was due to work on the milk run early next morning, went home. At about 11 p.m., Jack, keen to know where his eldest son was at that time of night, paid the half sleeping Prep a call, and learnt that John was at the Girl Guide camp.

Jack drove right into the middle of the camp, blew his horn and told the Guide leader. A search of the tents ensued, but John, when he heard the horn, bade good night to the Guides, scurried back over the railway bridge, collected his bicycle and was safely in bed well before his father returned.

Fireworks, now banned for private use throughout most of Australia, were then readily available in a country town for about four months each year. From almost as soon as John could walk, the two major attractions of the corner shop were lollies and fireworks. They were not expensive, particularly for a boy who had a ready income stream from about age 11.

Some of those fireworks were extremely powerful. Many boys and some girls lost hands and eyes and many others narrowly escaped being maimed. As John recalls, it was nothing to place a can over a bunger and blow the can metres into the air. It was routine for children to destroy people's letterboxes using fireworks.

As well as these random acts of vandalism, there were traditional family bonfires, replete with skyrockets that lit the night sky and occasionally set fire to the neighbourhood. There were many other types of fireworks, including the little jumping jacks that could chase people around their yards.

The headmaster made the mistake of attending a Scout bonfire. Dressed in a suit, he soon became a target for John and his mates, who tossed bungers at him every time he turned his back. The suit became singed and the Scouts' parents paid for a new one.

There was a big, tall kid in class, who we think ended up running a branch of Hells Angels. He by pulling apart five or six of the large bungers and combining the contents, he could make one huge bunger. It would be placed strategically in the boys' toilet block. Shortly after the bell summoned the students to assembly, John would light the long fuse then stand innocently in the assembly waiting for the explosion. On one occasion two teachers, checking the toilets to be sure no one was hiding to escape assembly, were violently shaken by an explosion.

Fireworks were not just for school or Wellington. At the cadet camp at Holsworthy, New South Wales, at the Scout jamboree in Victoria, crackers were part of the entertainment. Before one cadet camp, when Jack was showing his son how to pack a kit bag, he found a supply of three penny bungers sewn into John's great coat. Undaunted, John simply bought more to replace the confiscated supply.

Some were deployed during the train trip to Sydney. Leaving each station, John and his mates would toss a few onto the platform as a farewell to the stationmaster.

One of John's victims was the ute driver we introduced on the first page. He had travelled only about 20 metres before the bunger exploded amongst his fuel drums. John was a fast runner, but not as fast as the driver, who caught him, intent on taking him home to his father. As usual his good luck came to the rescue. Well aware of the thrashing that awaited him at home, he wrapped his arms and legs around a Kurrajong tree that just happened to be alongside.

Unable to prise him off, the driver went to the Mackay home and reported the incident. No doubt there was some punishment or at least a lecture but John's memory of that is less clear than of the incident itself.

Once, he and Bushy Bell found a small shed. The boys had no difficulty opening the locked door and inside found fuses, caps and dynamite. Undeterred by the sweating of the dynamite, which can make it unstable and prone to explode at the slightest disturbance, they used it to fell some trees.

After using up all the dynamite, they stored the remaining caps and fuses under Bushy's mattress. Mrs. Bell, described by John as "a highly volatile person", found the stash. Convinced that someone planned to blow up the house, she phoned the police, who confronted the boys. John and Bushy naturally knew nothing and the mystery of who intended to blow up the Bell house went unsolved.

On one of their rabbiting missions the weather was hot, the dogs were tired and rabbits were scarce. At the top of a range they came across five or six boulders, each about half the size of a car, perched precariously. The boys were quickly able to loosen the soil that held one in place, and with a little more effort they levered it free.

The boulder thundered downhill, crashing over and through trees and making a terrific noise. Well pleased with their effort, they sent another four or five of these missiles crashing down the hill.

When they got down the hill to admire their handiwork they found, somewhat to their consternation, that the boulders had crashed through a fence and had come to rest in the middle of a wheat crop. Exercising discretion, they did not wait to explain to the farmer how the boulders had slipped their moorings and landed in his crop.

Cadets from the age of 14 were sometimes allowed to take their .303 rifles home, but in the interest of safety, they weren't allowed to take the rifle bolts or ammunition. Bushy's father had a .303 and the boys had no difficulty taking its bolt and ammunition from his shed. "So as 14 year olds, we weren't mucking around with slug guns. We were shooting kangaroos with a .303 rifle."

Sale of the skins of shot animals was a source of income and firing the rifle a source of entertainment. Yet John knew several boys who were killed doing exactly what he and his mate were doing with rifles. Accidents had been caused by rifles discharging as someone climbed through a fence.

Much of young John Mackay's behaviour was risky and it took a huge element of luck to survive unscathed. He believes he knew how far he could push his luck, and that belief followed him into adulthood in his work: he would take what others believed was a huge risk, though he did not see it as huge.

Anne, the eldest Mackay sibling, left school and Wellington when John was about 15. All of the family went to the railway station to see her off to Sydney to begin a career in nursing. John has a clear recollection of the night. The memory is clear, partly because of his sister's leaving but especially because of a near tragedy for which he still blames himself.

He had been made responsible for Lizzie, the youngest Mackay, who was in a stroller. The train was moving and John, distracted as he gave a final wave to Anne, turned to see the stroller rolling over the edge of the platform. The front wheels were over the edge and Lizzie's head was against the train. He or someone, he is not sure, grabbed the stroller and Lizzie, who could so easily have been killed, was not injured. This did not prevent their father's swearing even louder and longer than usual.

Lizzie had several other close shaves in John's company. She was on the back of a horse, ridden by John, that bolted and they both nearly came off several times on a rough road over two kilometres. Then, while driving Lizzie to Orange to catch an aeroplane, they took a wrong turn. So, running late and again at high speed, John slid the car off the road and collided with a guidepost just a few hundred metres from the airport.

John and Anne remained close after she left Wellington. On one of his visits before she married, he travelled overnight to Sydney then took a taxi to her flat in Manly, only to find she was not at home. It was about 6 a.m. and having waited on the footpath for some minutes he noticed an open window on the second storey. With little effort he climbed to the window and let himself in.

Having helped himself to some breakfast he answered a knock at the door. A young woman in nurse's uniform asked if Sue was at home. She was not so John chatted to the visitor until another woman let herself in. They all chatted for a while, then John asked when Anne would be home.

"Oh, she lives on the floor below."

On the assumption that he would shortly leave school, John sat for the Intermediate Certificate examination, then conducted externally. At the same time he was applying for jobs, including a trainee draughtsman position at a nearby shire council. He considered a career in the army and his vocational counsellor suggested he would make a good plumber. . .

FIRST JOBS, FIRST LOVE

John Mackay drove his Holden to his first real job away from home, on a large cotton farm between Warren and Nevertire—Auscott. Workers were sitting around at the barracks when his white Holden with pink stripes along the sides and a huge flower on the rear window pulled up. From then on he was "Flower" or "Flower-power". This was, after all, the 1960s.

Eight months or so on the cotton farm were lucrative but a pretty tough existence. Typically he was picked up at 7 a.m. from the barracks and transported in the back of a utility with seven or eight other workers. Each was deposited at a piece of machinery several kilometres from anyone else. They would work throughout the day with no human contact except for the driver who delivered fuel for the machines.

John worked 11 hour days for seven days, then 13 hour nights for seven nights. Only when rain fell did the workers have time off.

He worked mainly on a bulldozer with about four hours' tuition. Workers were exposed to the widely varying climate. Summer, when John began, was extremely hot. Then the winter, particularly at night, was freezing. They mostly worked in the summer without shirts or hats. There was no "sun smart" campaign then and by the time he came home for Christmas, John's skin was almost black.

After a day on the dozers, almost completely covered with dust, the workers barely recognised each other as they tumbled into the utility to be transported back to the barracks. Industrial deafness from the machinery meant they couldn't hear each other for about an hour after finishing work.

In summer, with no air conditioning, sleep in the barracks during the day was almost impossible after the night shift. They commonly drove to the pool in Warren for a cooling swim and to sleep under the shade of a tree.

The work was hard and the boss could be demanding. One day, the boss picked John up after he'd worked from 7 a.m. to 3 p.m., so he could get some sleep before beginning the 13 hour night shift. It got worse. He was told if he had not finished the particular job by 7 a.m., "just keep going until you do." He finished at 3 p.m. the next day. It was a Saturday, so after a shower, he drove to Wellington and went out for the night.

The workers on the cotton farm, with few other employment options, were pretty tough. John was teased and bullied and got the occasional punch on the jaw. Having had enough he finally invited a big bugger to finish the fight outside, though he has little doubt he would have copped a flogging. "He didn't come outside and he never bullied me again."

John did prove quite popular at the many parties, because he had a record player and about 20 records. But the music died one hot day when he left his records on the back seat of his car and they all buckled.

At work one evening, a foreman came by, driving a three tonne Bedford truck erratically. The door opened and a very drunk Curly Murphy fell on to the ground. Ever responsible, John offered to drive his foreman with his supply of beer back to the barracks. Perhaps distracted by Curly's carry on, Mackay lost control of the Bedford, which went into an irrigation channel. The channel was more than two metres deep and the truck was almost submerged. Having reached the safety of the bank, John realised there would be serious questions over the large number of beer cans in the cabin. So he dived back in and recovered all of them.

Asked for an explanation the next morning, he created a story which omitted Curly Murphy. Whether or not his story was believed, he was reprimanded but, unexpectedly, not dismissed— a testament to his good work.

But the car crashes were a continuing story. In Wellington one weekend, drinking and playing pool at the Grand Hotel, Mackay and his mates heard about a party at the reservoir. When they got there, the grog had run out. So, with two passengers, John headed back to town on a mercy dash.

Going much too fast around a corner, the rear wheels slid along the edge of a cliff but did not go over. The car careered into a culvert, through a guide post and three trees, down a three metre embankment and back onto the road. The rear seat passenger was so drunk he was unaware of the crash which wrote off John's Holden and which could have killed all three. The only injury of note was a minor split lip sustained by his mate Louie.

"The police came out and the only question they didn't ask me was, have you been drinking?" It seemed the police officer was more concerned to find out how well a horse he had backed had gone. And John had to tell his mother that the car she had a half share in was a smoking wreck.

In those days, many young people thought little or nothing of driving when drunk. As long as John could find the car and start it, there was no impediment to driving and he wasn't about to stop driving fast. He knew others of about his age who were killed when driving in a similar manner

Not long after that crash, Jack wrote to suggest John could do much better than working on a cotton farm. There was a place called Canberra which offered opportunities that could be opened by sitting an examination called the Commonwealth Selection Test.

Canberra had some appeal. John's school friend, Dick Crockett, had already moved there. In February 1969 Crockett wrote: "Listen John, why don't you investigate a job with the Public Service down here. That's if you don't mind living in Canberra. You and I could have quite a stir." So he sat the selection test at a school hall in Dubbo and was offered a job in the public service.

The money was good at Auscott, so it wasn't an instant decision—but he returned to Wellington, and, with his parents, headed for Canberra. With Jack driving as though there was no tomorrow, the car came off the road for several hundred metres on a rough section near Cudal and became airborne. John, in the back seat, was amused during the short excursion off road to see the hat his father always wore stuck against the roof of the car. Jack had good driving skill and brought the car back onto the road with no damage to it or its occupants.

"So what do you do for an encore?" Betty asked.

He may have been a good driver in the bush, but Jack Mackay was not a city driver. After getting them in one piece to Canberra on the June long weekend in 1969, he had to take refuge on the median strip of Northbourne Avenue, having turned into the wrong side of the divided road to the city centre.

John's sister, Anne, visited the city at the same time, with her husband John. Eventually the family departed Canberra, leaving John Mackay in the unfamiliar surrounds of the nation's capital, standing forlornly outside Reid House, one of several hostels for newly arrived public servants. As his parents waved him goodbye, Betty was tempted to turn around and take her boy back to Wellington.

It was, after all, the first time this boy from the bush had been to Canberra. But it didn't take long to adjust to the communal living at Reid House, where he joined about 300 mostly young men and women, making their way in new jobs in an unfamiliar city. Living in a hostel which provided three meals daily had an appeal. There was a snooker room and several lounges where residents could watch television or play cards.

Room seven in A-Block was small, with few cupboards. But you don't need a lot of space to store a duffle coat, some moleskins, Beatle boots and six white shirts brought by your mother from an op-shop.

In the late 1960s, Canberra had a population of about 100,000, growing rapidly. Almost all of the young residents had come from somewhere else, so John was typical of people his age. It helped that Dick Crockett was already there, and John soon established a circle of friends.

Dick had followed his February prophecy of causing a stir with some practical advice in a letter of 1 June 1969. "For God's sake or your own, bring plenty of warm clothing when you come. It's shithouse weather that we are having. There is snow all around the surrounding hills and believe me, it's cold."

Reid House, close to the centre of town, known as Civic, gave its occupants easy access to the somewhat notorious Civic Hotel. It was a ready supply of cheap wine, close to a laundromat in East Row. Bachelors could slip across to the hotel for a few schooners while waiting for their week's washing to be done. Not far off, there was the Olympic bowling alley close to where the Olympic Pool remains.

So early days in Canberra were congenial—certainly a great deal easier than his work on the cotton farm—but there were, of course, some late nights. "I remember not going to bed at all one night before I had to go to work the following day. I might have been a bit untidy when I got to work."

Dick, who was working in the Australian Bureau of Statistics, introduced John and Rick Rossiter, who later shared a flat and became lifelong friends.

John's first job in Canberra was in the statistics section of the Department of Immigration. The office seemed to have come straight out of a Dickens novel. A supervisor sat on a raised platform at the front of the room and about 30 people worked at desks in perfect line and facing the front. The work involved coding passenger cards to produce statistics of new arrivals from overseas. In July 1969, there was an un-Dickensian interlude when someone took a television set into the office and all work stopped while the staff watched the first manned moon landing.

After only two or three months, the department gave John the opportunity to act as a clerk class 2/3. Others in the section of the same age and with more experience missed out because school leavers were not eligible to apply. Having worked for about eight months on the cotton farm, John Mackay was not classified as a school leaver.

So his pay doubled and life was good. Though he had always struggled with English expression, he was good at maths and efficient at producing immigration statistics. So he was regarded as an excellent employee. His life's goal then was to achieve the level of his supervisor, a clerk class four: "I thought to myself then, if I could ever, ever get her job, my life would be complete."

Life for Mackay could not last long without a car. Soon after arriving in Canberra, he bought this third car—another Volkswagen. In due course it would meet a similar fate to the Holden's but for the time being it provided transport for regular trips back to Wellington and to Sydney to see motor races at Warwick Farm.

An early revelation for the young man from Wellington was the wide range of food he had not previously tasted nor even heard of. This included pizza, and Chinese food far more extensive than the familiar curried prawns and rice of country cafes. His eyes widened further when, with the freedom of his newly acquired car, he went with a friend to Sydney to see a musical for the first time, the rock show, "Hair". Hair emerged from the hippie counter-culture and sexual revolution of the 1960s. Profanity, depiction of illegal drug use and a nude scene combined to make the show controversial.

In the Department of Immigration a job came up next door for an assistant forms officer to design the department's many forms.

At his interview John explained he had been good at technical drawing at school. So they asked him to re-design an existing form. The interviewers watched as he quickly produced a form which required eight parallel lines between two other lines. They had never seen this technique, which John had learned at school. "They thought straight away I was a genius. So I got the job."

Over the next two years, with a small team, he redesigned and catalogued about two thousand forms. He was good at the job and Immigration was so good to him that he considered making a career in that department. Then he realised he would not be sent overseas—as a clerk class five—until he was 25, and he was not prepared to wait that long.

Life in the public service, as outside it, used to be very different from what it has become. It was perfectly acceptable for staff to smoke at their desks and only since November 1966 had married women been able to hold permanent public service positions. For staff, particularly for new arrivals to Canberra, the public service workplace was the basis for most social functions.

Though breathalysers were introduced to Australia from about 1967, drink driving laws were less strict than now and random breath tests did not begin until the mid-1970s.

John Mackay was among those who drank lots at happy hours after work, then staggered to their cars and drove home. Even 20 years later, to his considerable embarrassment as he was by then a departmental deputy secretary, he had his licence suspended for driving under the influence of alcohol. The embarrassment could have been worse. The offence was in New South Wales and thus not publicised in Canberra.

His driving record was eventful. During the early days in Canberra he was caught speeding several times, which resulted in the temporary loss of his licence. He rolled the VW in Parkes Way. Later he ran it into a tree on his way to university. This might have been avoided had the car been roadworthy, but knowing its days were numbered he saw no point in fixing it. The foot brakes no longer worked but this country boy could use the gears to slow down, and when necessary the handbrake. Even after the handbrake failed, he continued to drive the car for some time with no major difficulty.

Running late for a lecture, he was speeding on Macarthur Avenue in O'Connor when a brand new Valiant came into his path from the right. Rather than plough into the side of the new car, he swerved off the road, dodged some trees and a fence and felt reasonably confident things would be alright. But in his path was a deep stormwater drain. Turning to avoid that, he crashed into a tree and was thrown through what remained of the windscreen.

Uninjured, except for a gash on his chin, he stood observing the wreck. His chin required stitches and he has a scar as a reminder of another fortunate escape from his driving exploits. In all he has seriously crashed about six cars, but at the time of writing he has not had a significant collision for more than 25 years. However cars he lent to his brother and his son were written off during these years, and he has had several amusing minor prangs. One involved a recent purchase, an expensive Jaguar that he really loved. With no one at its controls, it ran into a carwash at speed. And twice, after pushing the wrong button on the remote control, he has backed into the automatic gates at home. Overall the performance keeps improving, and as this book goes to press, his current car is intact.

Rick Rossiter was "a rich kid from Perth". He and John rented a flat on the corner of McCulloch and Carruthers streets in Curtin. Their culinary standards were not high. For two years they lived largely on pub food and takeaway meals. The small amount of home cooking was primarily of forequarter chops and tuna mornay. One exception to the standard fare came with a duck that Mackay won in a raffle. He approached with confidence the task of cooking the bird and all seemed to go well until it was being carved, when a plastic bag containing the giblets was discovered, still inside.

Next John shared a house in the outer suburb of Higgins with his friend from Wellington, Dick Crockett, and its owners, Dick's sister and her husband.

This move led to extra, probably unapproved, work for Mackay. The neighbour, David O'Brien, had a mowing and rotary hoeing business. Mackay worked for him on weekends and sometimes at night earning extra money doing landscaping work for which there was considerable demand in the rapidly growing national capital.

At about the same time, George Maselos, who had owned a corner shop in Wellington, was managing the bottle shop at the Captain Cook Hotel, popularly known as "the blood house", in Narrabundah. He arranged for Dick and John to work several nights each week behind the bar.

Working on forms at the Department of Immigration, it was often necessary to go up to the next floor to use a special micro typewriter in the typing pool. Despite being somewhat uncomfortable in an all female environment, John got to know several of the young women who worked there. At a work Christmas party at the Gundaroo Pub, he had a few dances and a few drinks with one of those women, Colette Carmody, and drove her to her home in Mawson.

They remained casual friends over the next few months. When Colette came to the all male forms office selling tickets in a 1971 Easter raffle, her presence did not pass unremarked, and John was able to say he had been out with her a couple of times.

Only after Easter did he find he had the winning raffle ticket. Upstairs he went to collect the prize—a huge basket of Easter eggs. One of John's principles was never to let a chance go by, so he asked Colette if she was free to go out on Saturday night. She was and they did. In March of the following year they were engaged.

The winning of the raffle introduced him to an organisation he would serve much later in his life. Had he won the second prize, a bottle of scotch whisky, no doubt he would have kept it. But the Easter eggs, particularly as Easter had passed, were of no particular value to him. So he took them to Koomarri, a school in O'Connor for disabled children. About 30 years later he would become honorary chairman of the Koomarri organisation, of which more below.

So in 1971, a somewhat shy young man from the bush drove his 1964 EH Holden, with its hotted-up motor and wide wheels, to the Carmody home in Mawson. Soon, dressed in his only good clothes, a pair of bell bottom trousers and a white polo neck jumper, he stood in the loungeroom surrounded by Colette's large Catholic family: her parents, Rex and Deirdre, and her seven younger siblings. Colette's sisters, Margaret, Paula, Bridget, Katie and Gina, were smiling and tittering at their sister's boyfriend. Her brothers, Robert and

Showing early promise of a successful drinking career, John celebrates his 21st birthday in 1971, with his sister Lizzie, and Colette, the girl he would soon marry.

Greg, fresh from working on an old car, were covered in grease and helped the bashful Mackay to relax. Colette's mother was an excellent cook. She told the young man who would later be her son in law that he could eat more food than almost anyone she had ever met.

While still new to Canberra and still really a naive country fellow, John turned up at work one morning with a dose of flu. A work colleague recommended his doctor, who had rooms in Dickson Chambers. John made an appointment but by the time he arrived he had forgotten the doctor's name. Feeling sure there would not be too many doctors in the Dickson Chambers, he checked the directory. "The first one I saw was Dr Barnardos. I thought, 'That will be him for sure'."

Inside the rooms he saw an array of charity collection boxes and thought it was a strange way to decorate a doctor's surgery. However, the confusion with the charity, Barnados, was soon rectified and he found the actual doctor.

5

BUILDING A HOME
AND A CAREER

1972 was a big year. John and Colette were engaged in March. John, although short of cash—he was paying off several cars, a couple of which no longer existed—bought a lavish engagement ring from a Sydney jeweller.

Also in 1972, he surpassed his life's goal of 1969, when promoted to clerk class five in the forms unit of the Department of Primary Industry.

He found himself working with some very bright people. This was the first time he had ever had people reporting to him. They were mostly young university graduates, yet Mackay had not even matriculated. One of his staff, a radical feminist who later became secretary of the National Party, told him in direct terms not to expect her "to make your fucking coffee".

He worked hard, but lacked confidence. When called in by the boss after three months, he expected a reprimand. Instead, he was told he was doing a great job and would act in a higher position. So he tried harder, which led to increasingly responsible jobs. "In no time at all I was completely out of my depth as an acting clerk class eight."

Aged 23, with no formal qualification, Mackay was sent for a few days to review the Department's Melbourne office, with a staff much older, and he supposed much wiser, than him. One was former test cricketer, Doug Ring. Mackay doubted that with his limited experience he could teach these people very much. Yet over the following three years he learnt much from the bright people around him. "I learned a lot about basic administration and management. I made mates at all levels of the Department. I learned to write reasonably well from an English workmate who had a degree in English literature. I basically copied his phrases."

He also made good friends in the regional offices. He hospitably invited about 20 of them home for a barbecue with virtually no notice to Colette. The barbecue turned into a pretty wild party and finished well after midnight. In the morning, five survivors shared a car to work and had to stop at least once while various people were physically ill.

Well before this inauspicious night, John Mackay and Colette were married on 30 September 1972. The wedding was held at the Daramalan Chapel and the reception at the Royal Canberra Golf Club.

Before dinner was served, Colette walked past a candle and her veil caught fire. She was rescued from serious burns by her father and her new husband. She recovered quickly, helped by a hairdresser on the guest list.

After a night in the honeymoon suite of the Canberra Rex Hotel, the newly married couple drove to Coffs Harbour in their almost new Mazda Capella. Upon their return they moved into a one-bedroom flat under a house in Aranda. There was so little room that dinner guests had to walk over the bed to get to the bathroom.

When Colette was pregnant with their first child, she resigned from the public service to work as a secretary with the law firm Snedden, Hall and Gallop. The job paid $5 more per week but the timing was unfortunate. A few weeks later, the public service introduced three months' paid maternity leave.

With a family, they would need a house. The first step was to attend a land auction at Canberra's historic Albert Hall. With no money for a deposit, and an upper limit of $3,000, John had selected several suitable blocks in Flynn. But he was outbid on all of them, so he bought a block he hadn't seen, a battle-axe block in Hedland Circuit, Flynn. Having written a cheque, he hurried to his real estate agent, Ray Anderson, of Grantham Homes, who gave him cash to cover his cheque. Then, using the land as the statutory deposit, he was able to get a loan to cover the cost of the land and house.

He introduced several mates to this method of obtaining finance and soon worked for Grantham Homes on weekends. He proved very adept as a real estate salesman and sold many homes in the growth areas of Belconnen and Weston Creek.

The Fraud Squad turned up after a couple of years, with questions about $60,000 missing from the trust account at Grantham Homes, pointing the finger at Anderson, Mackay, or both. Anderson went to gaol, while John, who'd had no involvement, was exonerated—but that was the end of a real estate career.

The Mackays were among the first people to live in Flynn. Their first child, Jane, was born in 1973. Their house, with sheets for curtains, for a while stood out like a beacon in what was then the most western suburb in Canberra. Their bed was the only furniture they owned and Jane slept in a washing basket.

John bought a second hand fridge, lounge and washing machine. Being colour blind, he had not realised the lounge was green. Neither had he seen having a fridge with a yellow and red interior as a problem. And his choice of a twin-tub washing machine did not appeal to Colette.

But they had established a home and developed close friendships with many of the new settlers. Most were in a similar position, with young children, a new house and garden—and no money. There were many communal barbecues, much beer and wine drinking and a good community spirit.

Life was, as John liked to say, an endless party. Several neighbours combined to travel regularly on weekends to Berriedale about 160 kilometres away, to buy meat. It was stored in chest freezers ready for the next barbecue. Though those families have since moved, they remain close friends.

The Mackays lived at the Flynn house for about 15 years, during which their son Ben and second daughter Claire were born. The house was extended and John added a deck. Neighbours helped each other with numerous home improvements, typically followed by a barbecue, well lubricated with alcohol.

After one morning's work at his house, John and two mates relaxed with a beer. Whether this caused the error of judgment is not clear, but the impulsive Mackay surveyed the unfinished work and decided there was enough time left in the day to lay concrete. A load of mixed concrete was duly delivered and the workers, by then not sober, set about laying it. Colette arrived home to see the three hard at work, shovelling and trowelling the mixture into place. Gravity then took its toll on one of the workers who fell face first into the concrete. The work was finished, but not without difficulty.

It would be a visitor who would outdo the shenanigans typical of the barbecues and parties in and around the Mackay residence. Colette's cousin and her husband George were visiting from Newcastle. The Mackays were looking after a neighbour's property while they were away. The day being hot, and after the requisite intake of alcohol, everyone repaired to the neighbour's property which had the considerable advantage of a fantastic above ground swimming pool.

George, who Mackay said was an absolute wild man, "even compared to us", began proceedings by doing summersaults off the top of the kids' swing before running across the lawn at high speed and diving into the pool. Each dive caused water to splash from the pool onto George's run-up. On about his

Beauty and the beast: Colette and John on their wedding day, 30 September 1972.

fifth demonstration of physical prowess, he lost his footing on the slippery surface and fell onto the wet grass about five metres short of the pool.

In a tangle of arms and legs, his momentum took him crashing into the side of the pool. Its wall was breached. First a trickle, then a gush of water collapsed the pool's wall, sending a wave of water surging across the yard, drenching garden beds and all the spectators.

Whether it was the trauma of crashing into the pool, or an excessive consumption of alcohol, at about 2 a.m. George passed out on the lawn of his hosts. They offered to convey him to the safety of their house but his wife insisted all he needed was a blanket over him just where he lay.

It should be recorded that they all made considerable efforts over the weekend to rectify, as far as possible, the damage to the pool and surrounds.

Another of the neighbours built a large shed which became known as the leisure centre. Neighbours, generally the men, met there on a Saturday afternoon to drink beer and play darts, pool or cards. On one occasion, after a barbecue, the blokes met in the leisure centre to play darts while their wives were left to clean up then wait for the game to end. It did not end until Colette, who John says was usually most tolerant, burst in and confiscated the darts.

Mackay's career continued to advance apace. In mid-1975 he was promoted to the Department of Prime Minister and Cabinet as a clerk class seven in the organisation and management section. His responsibilities included reviewing tasks and systems. He enjoyed working in this small but influential department, not least for its outrageous happy hours.

A series of standard replies were on hand to deal with the 200,000 or so letters sent each year to the Prime Minister. Occasionally people who were important, or thought themselves to be, would object to receiving a standard reply from the Prime Minister's office. To cope with this, a special standard letter would be sent to placate the offended constituent. As part of his review of this aspect of the Department's work, Mackay made a series of recommendations based on the more efficient use of electric typewriters which by then provided for the first time the ability to insert and delete text.

Mackay had an appointment for the afternoon of 11 November 1975 to discuss this matter with a staffer in the office of Gough Whitlam, the Prime Minister.

But 1975 was a momentous year for anyone working in the PM's department. Before going to the meeting, Mackay phoned to confirm the appointment, only to be told that the Prime Minister had been sacked by the Governor-General, Sir John Kerr, and the office was in chaos. Even a clerk class seven had no inkling beforehand that there was even the possibility Whitlam would be sacked.

He was, however, well aware of the serious situation facing the country in general and the public service in particular, caused by the Whitlam government's inability to have its appropriation bills passed by the Senate. As things stood, the Government would effectively run out of money on 30 November. All public servants were on notice that there might be no way of paying them after 30 November.

Not long after moving to Canberra, John had horrified his parents by saying he would vote for Gough Whitlam. "I was an unashamed fan of Whitlam." Despite the threat to his income, he was disgusted by the dismissal. He had a fond memory of a departmental ball at the Queanbeyan Leagues Club attended by Whitlam and his wife Margaret. They danced with everyone else and if there was any security that night to protect the Prime Minister and his wife, it was not obvious.

After the change of government following the dismissal of Whitlam, Mackay continued to work in the Department of Prime Minister and Cabinet under Prime Minister Malcolm Fraser. He became a clerk class eight and was on the weekend roster as duty officer.

Duties on the weekend roster included reading the incoming cables from

Australia's embassies around the world and phoning the appropriate senior officer if something was highly important or needed urgent attention.

"I learned a lot about how the bureaucracy worked—the power of PM and C. I made a lot of mates. We used to have the best happy hours of any place. We worked hard but we played incredibly hard."

Despite considerable emotion over the dismissal of Whitlam, the department, under its secretary John Menadue, maintained a professional neutrality after the change of government. "Menadue was an absolute class act in every sense of the word."

Mackay transferred to the Department's personnel section as an acting clerk class nine. This meant more access to senior people and opportunities to learn how the Department worked, what was important and what was not. He also gained excellent general administrative experience.

Duties included responsibility for staff at the Prime Minister's Lodge. One unpleasant task was to sack the Lodge's cook and this required him to visit the butler at about 11 a.m. The butler served a gin and tonic "that would put a horse to sleep". During the hour long meeting, they shared the contents of that gin bottle and negotiated the sacking of the cook in time for coverage of the event on that night's television news. Mackay's duties also covered the staffing of Government House. In that role, he and Colette were invited to the last official function at Government House for the Governor-General, Sir John Kerr. Despite Sir John's dismissal of Gough Whitlam, Mackay regarded the farewell to the Governor-General as a most auspicious occasion. He bought Colette a new dress and washed the car. "We both felt very special indeed as I pulled in under the portico and a man in a military uniform helped Colette out of the car."

Only a few weeks before the farewell function, Sir John had attended the Melbourne Cup on 1 November 1977, where, far from sober and widely booed and heckled by the crowd, he presented the cup to the connections of the winner, Gold and Black. Mackay recalls that Sir John was in a similar state on the night of the farewell function—dressed to the nines and drunk as a lord.

In February 1978, the Commonwealth Heads of Government Regional Meeting was held at the Hilton Hotel in Sydney. On 13 February a bomb exploded outside the hotel, killing two Sydney City Council garbage collectors, Alec Carter and William Favell. A police officer guarding the entrance to the hotel lounge, Paul Birmistriw, was fatally injured. Despite subsequent trials, mistrials, a Royal Commission and several related prison sentences, the perpetrator of the bombing has not been identified.

Many of John Mackay's colleagues were at the conference and he was also to have been there but was detained in Canberra.

Colette with Ben and Jane, visiting Jack at Wellington Hospital.

The world kept turning. The Shah of Iran, Mohammad Reza Pahlavi, was effectively overthrown in early 1979 after widespread demonstrations in his country the previous year. Before that momentous event, the Shah had written to Australia's Prime Minister, Malcolm Fraser. During a brief secondment to the Department of the Prime Minister and Cabinet's External Relations and Defence Division, working as a junior policy analyst, Mackay was directed to draft a response. Feeling quite inadequate as a policy analyst, he drafted a response which came back unaltered and signed by the Prime Minister. Despite this brief successful excursion into foreign affairs, Mackay remained convinced his career had no future there.

By the end of 1979 John's father Jack Mackay had been unwell for almost two years. John would visit him in hospital in Wellington and Sydney, and several times John and Betty thought they had said their last goodbye—only to arrive at the hospital the next morning to find Jack brightly sitting up and eating breakfast. Despite many nights sitting with Betty at Jack's bedside, John was elsewhere when his father eventually died in January 1980. It saddens him that he wasn't there to comfort Betty at the time.

6

ROUGH AND TUMBLE IN THE UNIONS

In 1975, having not matriculated, John Mackay was admitted to the Canberra College of Advanced Education, later the University of Canberra, as a mature age provisional student. In contrast to his previous attempt to gain a degree, this time he flourished with one high distinction, two distinctions and a credit in his first four units. Twelve months later he was no longer a provisional student. Only then did he realise he was far more academically gifted than his schooling in Wellington had indicated. The burden of his academic work was eased by Colette who often typed his essays and assignments late at night on the eve of the due date.

His success encouraged him to continue to work hard, but he was juggling part time study with increasing work commitments, a young family and a hectic social life. Then, in 1979, he was promoted to the Public Service Board as a clerk class nine. At the same time a letter came from the board congratulating him on receiving a scholarship that allowed him to study full time for 12 months on full pay.

With maturity, the lights came on and his degree in administration and economics included distinctions and high distinctions. He was awarded a prize by the Australian Institute of Management, for being the top student in Administrative Studies. "Something in me made me try to excel. I remember Mum was incredibly proud of what I had achieved."

During 1979 when he was away from work completing his degree, he was paid about $30 an hour by the university to tutor other students. He continued to tutor for the next five years and found it financially and academically rewarding.

Despite what had already been rapid progress in the public service, John attributes much of his later success to the part the University of Canberra played in his educational and personal development. On the university's 40th anniversary, he was asked to help pack a time capsule. He contributed a business card on which he wrote, "Thank you UC, you changed my life."

He was awarded an honorary doctorate in 2010, but has never used the title "doctor", believing that those who held honorary titles and used them were prone to auto-eroticism.

On his return to work for the Public Service Board he made new friends, including Allan Hawke and Ian Hansen, both of whom would further influence his career. But he did not enjoy his time at the board. "I had never thought much of the Public Service Board and once I was inside it I thought even less of it."

He was counselled several times for having too positive an attitude in trying to help government departments. The board then was effectively the central personnel authority which decided the resources allocated to each department. Mackay recalled that when working for the Department of Primary Industry he had to write to the board for permission to buy an office machine worth $200. "They just held enormous power and I didn't think they were very clever and they didn't use that power very wisely."

Whether apocryphal or not, the story is still told: when seeking a meeting with the chair of the board, a prime minister was told that he could come over at 3 p.m. the following day.

The board still had people who had obviously been given jobs immediately after World War Two. "It was a serious, serious boys' club and I couldn't get out of there quickly enough. I cheered from the sidelines when it was abolished a few years later."

So why work there? Well, the promotion meant more money and the opportunity to make valuable contacts and to learn how the public service worked. This part of his strategy greatly helped him to further his career in administration.

In April 1981, promotion as a clerk class 10 to the Department of Housing and Construction was another step up the public service ladder. Previously the Department of Works, it was responsible for the construction and maintenance of buildings and infrastructure in Australia and Papua-New Guinea. Much of this work was performed by its large trade workforce, which included carpenters, painters and plumbers. Its headquarters had moved to Canberra from Melbourne in the late 1970s.

Mackay was initially in charge of personnel policy, but that offered little challenge. When Warren Butler, who was always extremely busy and in high demand, was seconded to establish the First Home Ownership Scheme, Mackay begged to work in Butler's former role in industrial relations. He was given the job, which marked a major career change.

He was directly responsible for up to 40 staff and managed industrial relations for about 15,000 staff represented by roughly 30 unions at 300 sites across Australia. He was soon dealing with the tough building and metal workers unions—even the notorious Painters and Dockers.

Mackay had ambitiously sought a job with increased responsibility. On top of the industrial relations demands, he was overseeing important administrative aspects of major construction projects across Australia worth many hundreds of millions of dollars.

Before long the government embarked on a program to increase contracting out of construction and maintenance work, with corresponding reductions in the department's trade workforce. At the same time, the government wanted the department to reflect its industrial relations policy of containing costs. Mackay was soon flying around Australia to various work sites and managing numerous union claims, strikes and general industrial disputes.

The unions were concerned by a decision to close several departmental depots around Australia. This led to the department's New South Wales workforce marching down George Street, Sydney, late in 1981, led by left wing politician Tom Uren. Uren became a minister in the following Labor government and caused Mackay more than a little frustration and countless hours of work unravelling an industrial mess he set in train.

Mackay had to learn quickly while simultaneously resolving industrial disputes, alleviating work bans and keeping the minister and the departmental executive informed of progress. This was made easier by an excellent relationship with his manager Ross Pitt and Pitt's supervisor Bill Harris. Mackay said that both were incredibly bright and experienced people.

Mackay's knack with people served him well when dealing with the department's senior construction staff, led by Keith Rodda. And being able to turn most work commitments into social opportunities helped to establish good relationships with senior staff on frequent interstate trips.

Then the Australian Council of Trade Unions (ACTU) lodged a claim for a 38 hour week covering most of the department's workforce, who were already engaged in a widespread industrial campaign. ACTU official Jenny Acton called Mackay and invited him to attend a meeting next day in Melbourne to discuss the claim. Quite relaxed, he flew to Melbourne and went to the ACTU's headquarters.

Jenny Acton invited Mackay into a meeting room where he was confronted by a phalanx of about 30 national union secretaries. Feeling friendless, dressed in his three-piece suit and clutching his briefcase, he set about trading off the government's policy of reducing staff and closing depots against the unions' claim for a 38 hour working week.

Much of the subsequent negotiation occurred after hours in notorious union hotels in Melbourne. Some powerful union bosses were involved. As a principal negotiator Mackay sought an agreement with the unions that would suit both sides, but the Fraser government wanted to freeze all wages. Toward the end of the negotiations, he went to Melbourne for his first appearance in an industrial court. He read a book on how to be an industrial advocate, while flying to Melbourne on the day of the hearing. It must have been a good book, because the agreement was ratified in December 1982 by Sir John Moore and the full bench of the Conciliation and Arbitration Commission.

The timing of that endorsement proved crucial. Within only a couple of days the government's wages freeze, which would have sunk the deal, was introduced.

Despite the settlement of the 38 hour week claim, industrial disputes remained a major focus of the work. In 1984, the curse of asbestos became a major concern for health and safety and led to many disputes. One of these was over extensions to Sydney Airport terminal, where there was a rogue union delegate and some 25,000 square metres of roof space clad in asbestos. Another was over Sydney's Concord Hospital where kilometres of pipes were lagged with asbestos.

They were tough days, but not as tough as when the Hawke Labor Government decided to deregister the Builders Labourers Federation (BLF). The union, founded in 1911, marched under the slogan "Dare to struggle, Dare to win."

The union's demise followed a royal commission into corruption within the BLF. At about the same time its federal secretary, Norm Gallagher, was gaoled for corrupt dealings after receiving more than $150,000 in bribes in the form of labour and materials which he used on his beach house in Gippsland.

In 1984 while Mackay was up to his ears in industrial disputes, his boss, Tony Blunn, rang to say they were off to see the Minister for Housing and Construction, Stewart West. West, of the political left, was not keen on Hawke's decision to deregister the BLF, but wanted to be a player in the game.

The government's strategy comprised three components essential to deregistering the union—bullet proof legislation, support from the ACTU and support from the construction industry.

Mackay quickly formed alliances with a division head in the Department of Industrial Relations, Don McCallum, and Peter Medlock, senior private secretary to then Minister for Employment and Industrial Relations, Ralph Willis.

McCallum was responsible for preparing the necessary legislation and Medlock for gaining general union support for deregistering the BLF. Mackay's role was to gain the support of the construction industry, on which the department was spending hundreds of millions of dollars. This helped to prevent the construction industry from caving in to the BLF.

The first step was to deny government work to four major construction companies. These included Grollo and Herscu, both of which had been convicted of providing secret commissions to Gallagher and the BLF.

Not surprisingly, the loss of work worth millions of dollars and the Government's refusal to rent office space from companies that did deals with Gallagher or the BLF, prompted a response from those companies. Mackay was dispatched to Melbourne, in his three-piece suit and natty briefcase, to negotiate a deal.

There was no give and take. The companies had to renounce the BLF and agree to have no dealings with it. Only then would the department say publicly that the companies had joined the push against the BLF. Grollo agreed, but Herscu did not, instead making a successful takeover bid for Hooker Corporation.

Plans were well advanced for the new Tuggeranong Town Centre in Canberra's south, and Hooker Corporation had been shortlisted to bid for the development rights.

At about 1 am on the day of the land auction and still in the office of Stewart West, Mackay telephoned Tom Sherman, a senior lawyer in the Attorney-General's Department, to ask whether there were legal grounds to black list Hooker Corporation immediately and to disqualify Hookers from that day's auction.

Sherman's opinion was favourable, and after Mackay interpreted it to the minister and his staff, they agreed they stood on solid legal ground.

Hooker's representatives took their place for the auction in Canberra's Albert Hall. Shortly before it was to begin, Mackay and his men walked in and not so politely tapped these chaps on the shoulder and pointed out that they were disqualified from bidding.

This effectively brought the construction industry to heel. Companies recognised that if the government could disqualify the huge Hooker Corporation from lucrative work and get Grollo onside, there was no future in making deals with the BLF.

Phone calls protesting against the disqualification of Hookers reached the Prime Minister's office, demanding that Hawke curb these mad bureaucrats. Of course, it was Hawke's clear intention to put Gallagher and the BLF out of business and the howls of protest achieved nothing. Herscu caved in soon after, and the government had struck a near fatal blow against the BLF.

Meanwhile, Mackay was drafting a code of conduct for the construction industry. The code was effectively an ultimatum which, if not observed, would result in offenders being blacklisted. Companies that cooperated were offered the carrot of financial assistance.

Around this time the government introduced a community employment program which hired young people who had been unemployed for a long time. In 1983 the Department of Housing and Construction had 1,500 trainees in the program. They worked as trades assistants on the understanding that they joined a trade union.

As part of the agreement with the unions, Mackay was to send them details of all of the people employed under the scheme. It was then up to the unions to agree among themselves which workers each union would cover.

Letters were duly prepared and all but one was sent to the relevant unions. The letter to the BLF was posted by Mackay into the wastepaper bin. By the time the BLF realised its letter had gone astray, all potential new members had been signed up by other unions. "I went through a world of pain. What I had thought was a smart move became a difficult problem. I had to sort out the ensuing industrial turmoil when the BLF realised it had missed the boat."

For all this, Mackay does not seem at all repentant over what he calls his "silly, smart arse" way of dealing with this matter. He met several times with Gallagher and his industrial organisers to discuss various disputes. Ultimately, Mackay believes he played the dirty game as well as Gallagher did.

He found Gallagher to be quite a gentleman but some of the union's industrial organisers were pretty rough.

Mackay was saved once by the width of the table when one of these organisers threw a punch. Occasionally, as in his school days, someone would remind John that he was not very big. But in general his dealings with unions, even the BLF, were not threatening. Later he did receive a death threat, but it was from a former staffer, not a union organiser.

Several times, when negotiating with the BLF, Mackay was told everything could be fixed with a bag full of money. "I never dealt."

Tom Uren was the federal member for Reid from 1958 to 1990. He was a tough, left wing, traditional Labor man, a former boxer who joined the Australian Army and served in the 2nd/40th Infantry Battalion. He served in Timor before being made a prisoner of war by the Japanese from 1942 to

1945. While a prisoner he worked on the infamous Burma-Siam railway and was later in Japan when the atom bomb was dropped on Nagasaki.

Uren was Minister for Local Government and Administrative Services from 1984 to 1987. During that time the government decided to build Commonwealth offices in Parramatta. Supporting the aim of decentralisation, Uren decided that the building would be increased from 10 to 20 storeys. That meant the building would be much larger than it needed to be, so it was decided that staff from the Department of Housing and Construction, then accommodated in Australia Square in central Sydney, would be transferred to the new building in Parramatta.

Many of the professional staff to be transferred were living in Sydney's eastern suburbs or on the North Shore, and moving to Parramatta created its own industrial turmoil. This time Uren was not leading the protest.

Though Stewart West was also on the political left, he did not get on well with Uren. He was persuaded by his senior staff, including Mackay, to oppose Uren's decision to transfer Housing and Construction staff to Parramatta. West was in fact the most left leaning minister in the Hawke and Keating cabinets, yet he and Keating did get on well, even though Keating was from the New South Wales right—confirming that politics can be an unpredictable and quirky business. The row between Uren and West occupied several meetings of federal cabinet, where it received more attention than the nation's economy or defence. Ultimately, Uren won and Mackay was responsible for sorting out the mess that followed.

He met with union representatives in Sydney, where they agreed that people who did not want to move to Parramatta could be transferred to other departments. Further, people working in other departments and living in Parramatta would have the option of transferring to Housing and Construction in the new building.

Some staff, accepting that they had no choice, sold their houses elsewhere in Sydney in preparation for the inevitable move.

Then, after a cabinet reshuffle, West became the Minister for Administrative Services and promptly decided that staff, instead of moving to Parramatta, would go to the Zenith Centre in Chatswood on the North Shore. There was uproar from staff members who had sold their houses almost in the shadow of the new building. Many were now living on the other side of town and could not afford to buy back into the North Shore.

Negotiations over relocating staff were almost concluded close to Christmas of 1987. At the final meeting in Chatswood, one of the union delegates had had enough and announced that the meeting had been a waste of time and he would leave. Mackay, who rarely loses his temper, decided a good tactic would be to pretend. "So I started shouting and screaming—and I lost my temper within about 30 seconds."

He was asked to leave the room while the union representatives had a discussion. When invited back about five minutes later, he was bluntly told the agreement would not be accepted unless some very minor changes were made to the text. The changes were made and the matter settled.

The combatants were physically and emotionally exhausted and wanted nothing more to do with each other. They all entered the same lift which promptly became stuck between two floors. The strictures of the confined space proved almost too much for everyone.

The settlement they negotiated included a Chatswood allowance for some staff, while others were given assistance to sell their new houses and to buy on the North Shore. Other sweeteners included a gym and a child minding centre in the new building.

The political battle between two left wing warhorses was over. The final irony of this upheaval and waste of public money is that all of those staff positions have since been abolished.

Though Mackay had some terrific tussles with the Builders Labourers Federation, he found the Clerical Officers Association could be just as rough. Some of their representatives focussed on destruction and not on solving disputes.

Ultimately, he preferred dealing with the construction and metals unions because it was clear where they stood. "It was often very easy to have a beer and sort it out."

Not only did the clerks unions play rough, they played politics with meetings. "They would meet you to death."

One of the legacies of Australia's most significant engineering projects, the Snowy Mountains Scheme, was an engineering consulting company, the Snowy Mountains Engineering Corporation (SMEC). It became an international business employing about 600 staff. Despite a major downturn in the early 1980s, there was little political will to move its headquarters from Cooma because the large enterprise was significant to the relatively small town. And Cooma, snuggled within one of Australia's most marginal federal electorates, was able to exercise considerable political muscle.

In the electorate of Eden Monaro, where every vote counts, Mackay was given the task of saving the corporation. With colleague Steve Arnoudin he drove off down the 110 kilometre Monaro Highway from Canberra to Cooma, to meet the senior executives of the SMEC.

On the way a police officer clocked the car at 135 km/h. Assuming or hoping the officer was from Cooma, John said they were running late for an appointment to save the SMEC. He was admonished and told to slow down, but not booked.

About ten minutes later came the wail of another police siren. This time the recorded speed was 126 km/h. Having succeeded once John tried the same defence, well aware that some police officers' wives worked for SMEC in Cooma.

Sensing the case for the defence was not going well, Arnoudin flicked open a file that included words such as "urgent", "confidential", "minister", and the phrase, "future of the Snowy Mountains Engineering Corporation". The officer put his notebook away, delivered another admonition and told both public servants he did not want to see them again.

As they drove away, Arnoudin said he had two things to say. Firstly, he asked why John had told the second officer of the encounter with the law only ten minutes earlier. John argued this had set a precedent for not being booked. John asked what the second thing was and Arnoudin exclaimed, "For Christ's sake slow down."

They managed to save the SMEC but at a price. Around 60 per cent of the staff still lost their jobs.

In 1987 the Government merged the Departments of Housing and Construction and Local Government and Administrative Services with various sections of about five other departments. There was a huge clash of cultures and lots of jockeying for positions. Mackay prevailed as the branch head in charge of industrial relations for the new department.

While seriously involved in negotiating a new enterprise agreement, he was invited to a conference of up and coming managers at Batemans Bay on the south coast of New South Wales. This coincided with a visit by an exchange officer—a prim and proper woman from London. Mackay offered her an opportunity to see the coast. He drove rapidly along the notoriously dangerous Kings Highway, which links Canberra to the coast. Even 20 years later, at the time of writing, the road remained sub-standard, as did two other major roads into the nation's capital.

Undaunted by heavy rain, John terrified his guest with a rapid descent on the twisting Clyde Mountain road, occasionally drifting sideways around the tight bends with heavy rain still falling. Nevertheless, they arrived safely at the conference, which Mackay addressed on industrial relations and personnel management.

To illustrate the way things were headed, he distributed a draft agreement being negotiated with the unions.

Next day, the departmental secretary, Graham Glenn, also addressed the conference. Glenn, a former Public Service Board executive with considerable industrial relations experience, told the conference of the major agreement being negotiated with unions. So delicate were these negotiations that he could not possibly share the confidential draft agreement, of which he brandished a copy. One of the participants helpfully told Glenn that Mackay had distributed it the previous day.

In contrast to Mackay's parents, for whom punishment delayed was punishment forgotten, Glenn did not react immediately but certainly did not forget. Mackay sought to avoid Glenn for a few days, hoping he would forget. Some time later, when it was no longer possible to avoid going into Glenn's office, the conversation began something like, "By the way, Mackay . . ." There followed what John describes as "a metaphorical boot in the balls."

Somewhat unrepentant, he retained the view that if he had knowledge, chances were he would share it. Despite the reprimand by Glenn, the premature disclosure caused no catastrophe.

Heavy rain had continued during the conference causing local flooding. On the way back to Canberra with the visiting exchange officer, John drove through some deep water and managed to get them as far as Bungendore where the highway became impassable. Determined to avoid any suggestion of impropriety that might arise if they tarried on the lonely road, he took several drier detours to get them to Canberra.

The Mackays were happy living in Flynn, but as happens in the newer suburbs, some friends began to move. By 1988, they were both working in Civic and the family's financial position had improved. Their son Ben was due to begin high school at Daramalan College, run by the Missionaries of the Sacred Heart, in Canberra's inner north. So they considered moving to a more central location.

One of Colette's brothers recommended O'Connor. Having driven along Nardoo Crescent, they determined to buy a house there. A couple of days later, Colette went there with the two eldest children, who put leaflets in letterboxes saying, "I would like to buy your house."

With a keen eye on the future, the kids did not leave leaflets at any house in which they did not wish to live. The leaflets bore fruit and the Mackays negotiated on about three properties in the area, finally settling on a two storey dwelling at 16 Nardoo Crescent. It was an attractive house, well insulated, with magnificent cabinet work and an excellent view of the city. The view extended from Canberra's racecourse in the north almost to Parliament House in the south.

There was a self contained flat at ground level, which will become important in our story. Morning sun flooded the house, of considerable importance in Canberra's winters. The block was elevated, with the advantage of being above most of the heavy fogs that frequently plague Canberra in winter. "We just absolutely loved it," John says.

With interest rates for housing loans at about 10 per cent, and with an escalating salary, he was able to borrow about $200,000. It was not long, however, before interest rates shot up to about 18 per cent. "It almost sent us broke but we survived that and it was just a beautiful place to live."

A week or so before they moved in the previous owners arranged a welcoming function so they could meet other people from the neighbourhood. It was a wonderful gesture but to John it felt like visiting an aged people's home. One of the nearest new neighbours was a woman aged 100. The second youngest person was over 60.

"We just felt so young."

Claire, the youngest child, born on 5 June 1982, was promised that after the move she would go to St Joseph's Primary School in O'Connor. Her parents had assumed there would be no difficulty in an older suburb with an ageing population, getting Claire into the parish school.

Colette took her daughter to her new school, only to find there were no vacancies. The distraught child learned she would have to go on a waiting list and it might be quite some time before she could get in. Mackay arrived home to find his wife and daughter in tears.

"I thought, well, bugger this." He phoned the principal to explain the distress caused by the school's refusal. He went on to explain that he might just have to go to the Archbishop's House where he would camp on the front lawn until a vacancy came up.

A few hours later the principal phoned Mackay to say two things: firstly, that the Archbishop was not the slightest bit amused by Mackay's thuggery and threats and secondly, that his daughter could start on the following Monday. "I always felt pretty bad it was my thuggery which got her in there so we tried to do the right thing by the school at every possible opportunity."

The O'Connor house stood on a large, sloping block, replete with many trees. These included persimmons, magnolias, crab apples and dogwoods. In part to make better use of the land, and in part to combat the rapidly increasing interest rates, they divided the land so one of Colette's sisters could build a house there. "I had less lawn to mow and we had instant friends next door."

The Mackays stayed until early 2001, renovating the house considerably. About ten years after they moved to Braddon, another inner northern suburb, they still cherished the memory of the house in O'Connor.

7

DIFFICULT TIMES FOR
DIFFERENT SIBLINGS

Coming from a large family, it was almost inevitable that John Mackay's siblings would follow divergent paths and careers. There were signs of just how different those directions would be in the early teenage years of David, Mark and Stephen.

By then, John had observed that David and Stephen were more effeminate than their brothers and that Mark was incredibly rebellious. It is possible that numerous accidents, including his being dragged along by a horse and being struck in the head several times by various missiles, contributed to Mark's unruly nature. While still a child he had several fits and was found to have scar tissue on his brain. His education, always limited, ceased when he was expelled from school. Erratic driving cost him his licence and eventually led to a short time in Bathurst gaol.

The day of his arrival in the gaol coincided with one of the riots in the 1970s that ultimately led to the Nagle Royal Commission, which sat from 1976 to 1978. When Mark was released, John, who had recently moved to Canberra, tried to set his younger brother on a better path. He found Mark a job as a gardener and Mark proved so adept that he was transferred to Government House. That job ended when a security check revealed his prison record.

Mark then lived in Sydney, supporting twin sons and a heroin addiction. He robbed four banks, stole cars and ultimately spent about ten years in prison.

On 8 December 1979 *The Daily Telegraph* reported charges against Mark. The headline proclaimed, "Heroin Addict behind Four Hold-ups, Court Told". His targets were Commonwealth Banks at Castlecrag, Northbridge, Willoughby and Edgecliff.

Mark told John afterwards that when he was arrested he was handcuffed and taken to a small room where he was interrogated by a notorious member of the New South Wales Police, Detective-Sergeant Roger Rogerson. With his face almost touching Mark's, Rogerson, breathing garlic and grog, demanded to know where Mark had hidden the money. In response, Mark headbutted Rogerson, who promptly retaliated by giving Mark a good kicking.

Rogerson was dismissed from the Police on 11 April 1986 and later convicted of perverting the course of justice over $110,000 deposited by him in bank accounts under a false name. He served nine months in gaol in 1990 and a further three years from 1992 after his appeal was dismissed.

While Mark was in prison, John persuaded the New South Wales Minister for Corrective Services, the late Rex Jackson, to allow Mark to be released for Christmas. Jackson was later found guilty and gaoled in a completely unrelated case of accepting a bribe of $12,000 in 1983 and of conspiring to organise the early release of three prisoners from Broken Hill Correctional Centre.

After Mark's eventual release from prison, John tried hard to help him. He allowed Mark and his twin sons to live in the O'Connor house and found him several jobs. Mark repaid this by stealing from his employers and writing off a couple of John's cars.

On one occasion while John was still in bed, Mark asked to borrow his car. Minutes later Colette and John heard the crash as the car was destroyed.

Later, Mark succeeded in persuading John that he needed a car to rescue one of the twins from a Tuggeranong house, which the son was sharing with some highly disreputable people. Mark, angry that his son had run away, returned about 90 minutes later with the boy, who was sporting a fresh black eye. Mark said that when he arrived at the house, armed with his father's Samurai sword and a baseball bat, he had used the bat to pacify the man who opened the door. Then he brandished the sword, instructed everyone else not to get out of bed, grabbed his son and left. About 100 metres down the road he stopped the car, gave his son a good smack in the eye to remind him not to keep bad company, and headed home to O'Connor.

On another occasion, when Mark was living in a flat in Canberra, he phoned John seeking help as about eight men were threatening to break down the door and belt Mark with baseball bats. John phoned the police and left the protection of his brother to them.

One day at an inner city service station Mark, who was never far from

At John's and Colette's home in Flynn in 1976: from left, John with siblings Lizzie, Philip, Mark, Stephen, David and Anne.

trouble, provoked another customer who promptly drove out onto the road, backed in through another entrance and ran over Mark.

Mark has survived it all and lives in Newcastle. John occasionally sends him money and even financed a car for him. Mark went on a methadone program and gave up heroin.

John describes his own personality as highly addictive and says he has not dabbled in drugs. He knew what the consequences would be if he did.

Brothers David and Stephen also became heroin addicts. John and Colette at various times allowed David and Stephen to stay at their house. They lent both money, which was not repaid. John guaranteed a loan for David and ultimately repaid some two thousand dollars, a considerable sacrifice to a young family.

Shopkeepers would come to John's house seeking payment for dishonoured cheques, which resulted from one or other of the brothers having stolen cheques from John's cheque book.

John and Colette had brought Stephen to Canberra and enrolled him in Belconnen High School. John later found Stephen a good job and helped him to buy a car, but Stephen smashed the car and lost the job.

John is philosophical over his ultimate inability to help both brothers: "I don't think I ever understood enough about heroin and the life they were leading to seriously help them. I thought I could just buy them out of trouble, but you can't."

David was among the first people in Australia diagnosed with AIDS. This was a pretty tough time for John and the family. Like most Australians at that time, he knew little of the condition. It was before the 1987 television advertising campaign that depicted the Grim Reaper in a bowling alley, knocking over men, women and children as ninepins representing AIDS victims. The advertisement, aimed at raising awareness of AIDS, was part of a $3 million campaign by the National Advisory Committee on AIDS.

Some prominent church people increased the stigma of AIDS by suggesting it was God's punishment of homosexual people and drug addicts. In conservative Wellington, where their mother still lived, that opinion was fairly common. With few people who had genuine sympathy for her two sons dying from AIDS, Betty had a terrible time.

John, raising young children and with increasing work responsibilities, had become estranged from both brothers. As David and Stephen became seriously ill, John and other siblings supported their mother. "We did our best to support Mum while they went through this hideous death." John and Anne accompanied their mother when she visited David and Stephen in Sydney and later drank heavily as their way of dealing with it.

One of those days remains vivid in John's memory: "One Sunday morning late in the piece I went with Mum to St Vincent's Hospital and we put David in a wheelchair and I wheeled him over the road to the hospice to say his last goodbye to Stephen."

Both brothers were emaciated and both understood they were close to death. And John had his distressed mother on his arm. In what was clearly an understatement he said, "It was a really emotional day."

After parting from his mother, John went to Sydney Football Stadium to see the Canberra Raiders play South Sydney. Instead of catching up with his mates, he sat in the rain on his own.

"I didn't have much cash on me so I thought the best way to drown this pain was to drink schooners of white wine. I probably had half a dozen of those—sitting in the rain feeling pretty bloody sad about the whole tragic day. I'll never forget that day as a way of trying to wash away some of the pain of seeing two of your brothers who were soon going to die."

They died within six weeks of each other. John regretted not having understood better, but he did not blame himself for their deaths. "I did make a pretty serious attempt to help them—Mark, Stephen and David—at various stages. But obviously that help fell short of what was required."

He doesn't believe the experience made him a better father. He says that when his children were growing up, he was at least as focussed on building his career as on being a great dad. His three children left Canberra and later returned. At the time of writing they live close to their parents and all were getting on well. "In my case I think that is most undeserved. In my wife's case I think it is very, very well deserved. She was a great mother. I doubt I was a fantastic father."

But the death of two brothers certainly had a long term effect: "I think it has made me much more compassionate than I would have been."

This compassion was in evidence one night when John was halfway home from a corporate dinner and became tired of walking. He decided to take a taxi that he saw depositing a passenger. A delay ensued, so John asked the driver what was wrong. The driver explained that he could not find anywhere for his passenger to stay.

John phoned Colette to say they would have a Japanese house guest for the night. His wife was horrified and the guest protested that he was Korean. When they got home, Colette made the man welcome and all spent a comfortable night.

FROM POLITICS
TO PROPERTY

I n 1989 a major restructure of the Department of Administrative Services included various amalgamations. In the ensuing tussle for senior positions, John Mackay prevailed as head of industrial relations, and later, to acting first assistant secretary, management.

He felt he was doing a fantastic job and when interviewed for the permanent position in April, he understood that it would be his—as did the two deputy secretaries who interviewed him.

But almost immediately, the departmental secretary, Graham Glenn, was transferred and Noel Tanzer took his place as the new secretary of the Department of Administrative Services. Tanzer brought with him a first assistant secretary, Paul Taylor, from his former Department of Social Security, and the promotion was cancelled.

This terrible disappointment lasted about one day. Then Stewart West, Minister for Administrative Services, invited Mackay to be his senior private secretary.

The senior private secretary is a key link between the minister and all areas of the department as well as other ministers' offices. The Minister and his new secretary had already established a close working relationship during the industrial skirmishes over the deregistration of the BLF and this good relationship continued until West lost his portfolio in 1990 to Nick Bolkus.

Stewart West, the only minister from Labor's left faction in the first Hawke

Light relief from the heat in the kitchen: posing in 1990 at the desk of the Minister for Administrative Services, Stewart West, when he was West's senior private secretary.

cabinet, initially served as Minister for Immigration and Ethnic Affairs. He resigned on 4 November 1983 over a cabinet decision on uranium mining. He was reappointed to cabinet on 3 April 1984 as Minister for Immigration.

West remained in cabinet for the Hawke Government's next two terms as Minister for Housing and Construction from 1984 to 1987, and Minister for Administrative Services from 1987 to 1990.

West's somewhat strange appearance was exaggerated by thick spectacles. He was frequently uncomfortable with the right-wing-dominated cabinet.

With a little experience of the Minister's mannerisms it was possible to predict quite accurately when he was about to explode with rage. He could be volatile but was generally calm. When an outburst came, West would often dart into the bathroom to cool off.

Mackay liked and greatly respected West, although he thought West was perhaps too diligent for his own good. Mackay would skim the enormous volume of briefing papers, but West would generally read every one thoroughly. Most politicians left Canberra soon after Parliament rose. But West would remain in Canberra or elsewhere away from his electorate of Cunningham for many days, attending to ministerial business. As a result, he lost preselection and was replaced by Stephen Martin as the candidate for the 1993 election.

Working for West brought a much better understanding of the relationship between government and public service. Though generally the operation was effective, disagreements even within the same department could end up with the Minister having to sort things out. Sometimes two briefing notes came for the Minister from the Department that reached opposing conclusions. Mackay would return these to the Department with advice to sort out its conclusion. Twelve months in that adrenalin fuelled job seemed much longer. It was always necessary to take action, to work day and night, understanding or interpreting the Minister's needs and wishes.

John loved the work but recognised from the outset that the hours required to do it well could cost him his marriage unless he and Colette found an effective way of communicating. So he promised her he would walk with her for an hour every day at 6 a.m. regardless of how late he got home or in what condition. It was a promise he rarely failed to keep. He also came home for dinner almost every night before returning to the office. They still go on daily walks together.

In later years, on their regular walks to the peak of Mount Ainslie, he would often stop to do some mobile networking with leaders who also happened to be out and about, including Catholic and Anglican bishops, the Commissioner of the Federal Police, the President of the Australian Rugby Union and the Auditor-General. He has also done frequent early morning radio interviews while out walking, including talks with Ian "Macca" McNamara on his Sunday morning ABC program "Australia All Over".

While working for Stewart West, John had to take a lot of responsibility for his brothers, David and Stephen, who were dying from AIDS. West gave him time to travel to Sydney, where his brothers were in hospital. "He and everybody else in the office were very sympathetic and saddened by my plight."

With the pressure of work and his brothers' ill health, John coped by applying his management skills to himself. To some extent, it was enjoyable being under stress and at the centre of attention. Most of all, he enjoyed showing that against all odds he could deliver the desired result.

Under all the pressure John was almost caught with his pants down. After rushing the previous night to Sydney for a morning engagement to be attended by the PM, he woke to find he had taken the trousers of one suit with the jacket of another. Fix-anything-Mackay phoned Colette. He arranged for her to send the other half of his suit with a colleague travelling from Canberra to the function, assuming his colleague would bring the jacket to match the trousers.

Instead, with only minutes to go, he received trousers to match his jacket. He scurried into an unoccupied lift and set about changing his strides. To ensure privacy he pressed the stop button to keep the doors shut.

Changing trousers, while still wearing shoes, with one hand busy pressing a button is difficult. But the potential for exposure to the assembled crowd and Bob Hawke was motivation to make the task possible.

On another occasion he had to deliver a keynote address to a conference of occupational hygienists in the Blue Mountains. After driving from Canberra on a Sunday, dressed in shorts and thongs, he had a huge night out and awoke not feeling well. When he was about to be introduced to the audience he glanced down and noticed all too late that he was wearing odd shoes. At least he had a left and a right—each on the correct foot.

When truck drivers with a grievance laid siege to the Parliament in 1989, the building was effectively surrounded by semi-trailers, and cranky truckies demanding to see the Minister. Mackay was asked to arrange a meeting, but as the Minister was away, he had to go down, with little knowledge of the cause of the truckies' grievance, and assure them their concerns would be passed on. His major concern was that it being a Friday with Parliament not sitting, he would appear not wearing a tie on that evening's television news.

Managing the seven or eight staff in the Minister's office had its challenges. Some were political appointees with little regard for administration. Some ran their own race much of the time and one in particular was as bright as he was erratic. Even some of the political appointees were more focused on the agendas of other ministers than on West's.

One staff member, Harold Thornton, brother of actress Sigrid Thornton, occasionally went missing. One morning when he failed to arrive, it turned out he had decided at midnight to drive to Queensland to see his girlfriend. Another time West rang Mackay in Sydney demanding to know where Thornton was. Here with me said John, and asked whether West wanted to talk to him. It was lucky the answer was no, because Mackay had no idea where Thornton was.

On a much more serious matter, bracing himself for a ministerial outburst, Mackay sidled into West's office to say that his former senior private secretary, Michael Ross, would the next day attend the NSW Independent Commission Against Corruption (ICAC) to answer allegations of corruption, including some involving Commonwealth property while working in West's office. Mackay previously had doubts about Ross, not least over the number of times he had been bashed.

Ross featured in a 1990 ICAC report of its investigation into North Coast land development. The Commission found the trust account of a Tweed Heads real estate agency was being used to launder money from a land development consultant, Dr Roger Gareth Munro. At the direction of Tweed Shire Council Deputy President, Thomas Edward Paul Hogan, $5,000 of $20,000 from the trust account was paid to a Canberra bank for the benefit of Ross.

A consultancy business run by the chairman of the North Coast Industry Development Board, Barry John Cassell, had a shareholder or partner named Michael Prince. Cassell told the Commission that Prince was the pseudonym of one Michael John Ross, a federal public servant and former state ministerial staff member. Cassell acknowledged that the false name had been used to conceal improper payments to Ross for assistance he was giving to the Cassell consultancy business. This was the very same Michael Ross as the one to whom money had been paid by Councillor Hogan.

The Commission found Cassell took advantage of Ross's access to federal government information after his move to Canberra in 1983. This led to Ross's assisting Cassell with business migration matters and to Ross's leaking confidential information to Cassell about government property. At relevant times, Ross was working with the Minister for Immigration, the Minister for Administrative Services, and the Australian Property Group within the Department of Administrative Services.

Ross left West's staff on 13 November 1987 and joined the Commonwealth Public Service on the 30th of November that year. Initially on a contract, he obtained permanency under the Australian Public Service Act on 21 December 1988.

When he first gave evidence before the commission, Ross was an administrative service officer class 8, working with the Australian Property Group within the Department of Administrative Services. He resigned during the investigation after evidence of his involvement in Cassell's consultancy business was given before the ICAC.

Meanwhile, West's office, with the aim of improving the Labor Party's electoral prospects, helped develop a plan to ban all political advertising on television. The key Labor Party officials, the Prime Minister's office and the Australian Democrats had given support in principle. Only five extremely sensitive numbered documents detailed the plan.

But when West, Mackay and Thornton went to see the Prime Minister to outline the scheme, Bob Hawke rejected the plan outright, stating in expletives that it would be a disaster, and sent his visitors away.

Back at the office, West ordered the shredding of the five confidential documents to avert the risk that they could be leaked and cause political embarrassment. Mackay and Thornton fed the four documents they held into the office shredder, then assured West that none of the documents remained.

However, they were well aware that the Australian Democrats had the fifth copy. So Thornton went to their office with the unlikely concocted story that the minister's office did not have a copy of the document and would they mind very much if he borrowed theirs to make a copy. Naively the Democrats handed their copy to Thornton who ran out the door with it. In all likelihood, he still has it.

There was a mistaken image, particularly outside Canberra, that parliamentary staff and public servants in the capital were detached from reality and spent a dreamy life contemplating their navels. Even if this were true of some, it was not the reality for those in senior positions. A hands on approach sometimes meant getting those hands dirty with the grime of politics. If John Mackay ever had time for a dreamy existence, it would soon be shattered, as it was when he took a phone call to be told Treasurer Paul Keating wanted to speak with him. Many in Canberra experienced Keating's invective. Such an encounter was not easily forgotten, John says, and the author can verify that from personal experience.

Even with the phone about 30 centimetres from his ear, there was no difficulty hearing the tirade: "I saw Keating as a charming man and a clever bugger. But when he blew he really knew how to turn it on."

During a particularly heated phone call with the great man, Mackay, who was giving as good as he received, realised the line had gone dead. Keating had decided to finish the conversation in person. He came storming down the corridor, and burst in snarling, "Listen, sunshine . . ."

The job was interesting and enjoyable, with considerable leeway and a great deal of responsibility. "I thrived on it," John says. "I loved it. Whatever the government was doing was exciting in those days."

What is more, he was part of it. He learned the inner workings of government and put that knowledge to use later, on his return to the Department from West's office.

The election on 24 March 1990 was to be Bob Hawke's last as Prime Minister. The Labor Party, with a swing of only 0.93% against it, lost eight seats and the popular vote, but retained government with 78 seats, just three more than required for a majority in the lower house.

In the lead up to the election, as had been anticipated, getting Greens preferences was critical to Labor's chances. A sticking point was a proposal to establish a gold mine at Coronation Hill in the Northern Territory.

The international price of gold had increased in the early 1980s and in 1984 BHP began drilling at Coronation Hill and soon obtained promising results.

The site for the proposed mine is now in the Kakadu National Park in the headwaters of the South Alligator River. Developing the former uranium mine as a gold mine was subject to Aboriginal land claims and the mine was opposed by the conservation movement generally and the Greens. Yet there was pressure on the government to allow the mine with its potential to generate hundreds of millions of dollars for Australia.

With Mackay, West chartered an aeroplane and flew to the area to speak with mining interests, conservationists concerned over the damage a mine would cause, and representatives of the traditional owners of the land, the Jawoyn people.

During the flight home, West came up with a proposal to at least defer approving the mine until after the election. His proposal, which included virtually insurmountable pre-conditions for mining, was put to the environment minister, Senator Graham Richardson, who was also a significant Labor strategist, conscious of the need for Greens preferences. He welcomed West's proposal and later acknowledged in his book *Whatever it Takes* the critical role West played in getting the Greens onside and winning the 1990 election for Labor. In 1991, the Government formally banned gold mining at Coronation Hill.

Before the 1990 federal election, West had gained cabinet approval to increase the parliamentary postal allowance, believing this would generally favour Labor, which had more MPs than the Coalition. The Liberal Party challenged the postal allowance increase and the High Court's the complex decision was handed down only two or three days before the election. It seemed to uphold the challenge and West's office was beset by journalists seeking his reaction. West was campaigning in Queensland, so Mackay issued a media statement on his behalf saying legal advice indicated the High Court had supported the increase and politicians could continue to spend the extra postal allowance.

Having read the Court's decision and Mackay's media statement, West phoned two hours later, to say it was clear he had lost and the statement must not be issued. Learning that it had been issued already, he was horrified that there would be uproar about the misleading statement. Mackay agreed but said they could get away with the deception until after the election, as they did.

Despite West's key role in the 1990 election win, after the election he lost his portfolio to South Australian Senator Nick Bolkus. This was a sad time for West, and for John Mackay. He says West had more to offer, but that his supporters would argue that as a former waterside union official from Wollongong with left wing affiliations, he had done well to have been part of the Hawke cabinet.

West lost his portfolio on the same day as Western Australian Senator Peter Walsh ceased to be Finance Minister. The two old warhorses from opposing Labor factions commiserated over dinner, reflecting on their achievements and speculating on their future. John was the only other person at that dinner: "It was just such a fantastic privilege to be with these two wonderful men. I appreciated at that very time just how special it was to be with them."

While they worked together, the Minister often accepted advice from his senior private secretary. So when Mackay picked up West the next morning, he strongly advised the former minister to be gracious when he faced the media, and to say things such as, "It has been an honour and a privilege . . ." and "Yes I am sad, but . . .".

John recalls his reaction. "He said I fucking won't be saying that at all. These bastards have cut me down and I am going to give it to them. And he did."

Enjoyable as the job had been, John admits that on the day in April 1990 that he left West's office, "I felt like a huge weight had been lifted from my shoulders and I had a great sense of freedom. I think this is because I had basically lived inside the walls of Parliament House for the previous 12 months. It was almost always exciting but was also a very closeted existence."

The success of departmental initiatives often depends on advice to the relevant Minister from the senior private secretary. Indeed, whether a submission even reaches the Minister can depend on the secretary's judgment. John Mackay's "can do" approach to his work had been valued by the Department of Administrative Services, and when he rejoined the department after the election he was owed some favours by senior departmental staff. The reward was what he believed to be the absolutely best job in the public service.

John Mackay was appointed general manager of the Overseas Property Group. To a man of 42, who had not travelled outside Australia, this appointment cleared the slate of any favours owed. It came as a surprise to the staff he was to supervise. They had not been told they were getting a new boss. On his first day he walked into the office and asked where he would find the general manager's office. Mackay's predecessor was on sick leave and he was told the general manager was not there.

"He is now," Mackay told his staff. This appointment had nothing to do with his knowledge of other countries, nor his experience of managing major construction projects. His only construction experience was the family's three bedroom house in Flynn. He quickly realised that managing a billion dollar property estate with a multi-million dollar construction program in 70 countries would entail another sharp learning curve.

This learning was greatly helped by his new boss, department deputy secretary Tony Hillier, a former general manager of the Overseas Property Group. He said the job could not be done while sitting at a desk in Canberra.

With the Secretary of the Department of Administrative Services, Noel Tanzer, and the coat of arms for the new Australian embassy in Tokyo, in 1991.

"I never implemented a piece of advice with such enthusiasm."

John learned after 14 months in the job he had been dubbed Marco Polo by his staff. In little more than a week he was off to Hong Kong, Beijing and Tokyo. He inspected construction of two huge embassy complexes, both with dozens of staff apartments. The apartments were particularly popular with staff in Beijing, who, after the Tiananmen Square uprising, felt safe in a secure compound.

The uprising had begun in April 1989 after the death of former Communist Party General Secretary, Hu Yaobang, who was deposed after seeking political and economic reform. The student led uprising was put down on 3 and 4 June by the Chinese military with thousands of civilian deaths and injuries.

However the new apartments were unpopular in Tokyo, where staff had been living in expensive houses and apartments across the central business district of one of the world's most expensive cities.

During one of his numerous overseas trips, Mackay was laid low in Jakarta with a severe case of food poisoning. The department secretary, Noel Tanzer, was in town and the Saturday evening was set aside for a meal at one of Jakarta's finest seafood restaurants.

In his delicate state, Mackay had to miss out on that, not daring to stray far from the toilet in his hotel room. It was while so positioned he wrote a cabinet submission for the construction of a new Australian embassy in the Indonesian capital. The Finance Department had strenuously objected to the site of the proposed new embassy and John remains immensely proud of gaining cabinet approval, based on a submission written in a hotel bathroom.

That submission might not have been entirely fair. Photographs of the two sites were attached and the photograph John chose of the site preferred by the Finance Department was taken from an unusual angle which made the site look like a rubbish dump.

Much to the chagrin of Finance bureaucrats, the submission was endorsed by cabinet and the embassy was built where John Mackay wanted it. He had negotiated the land deal with President Suharto's second eldest son Bambang.

He went to New Guinea and by coincidence arrived in Port Moresby the day after an Australian soldier was shot dead while trying to defend his wife against the notorious "raskols", the local criminal gangs. The soldier had already handed over money and the keys to his car but resisted when the raskols sought to take his wife. He was then shot. Security in the capital was almost non-existent for locals and for people on overseas postings.

Mackay was horrified. Almost immediately he dictated a cabinet submission by telephone, which resulted in the construction of a compound for Australian High Commission staff, including about 50 apartments and a swimming pool.

This response to the endemic violence of Port Moresby demonstrated a consistent approach to problems that needed solving. He saw a need and promptly made a proposal that under normal circumstances could be considered an insult to the host nation. The acceptance of his submission confirmed Mackay's confidence in his ability to "crash through", using initiative to find remedies.

Staff working in Australia's overseas missions generally welcomed his arrival. He quickly learned how to tell whether those staff needed or wanted some improvement in their accommodation. One clear sign of an impending serious request was being paged by an ambassador while still on an aircraft or just after disembarking. If there was no early sign of an ambassador, the stay was likely to be uncomplicated.

Not every ambassador was hospitable. Richard Butler showed John around the residence of Australia's embassy in Thailand. It was about lunch time and Butler showed his guest the dining room but there was a place set only for one. "It would never have occurred to him to say, 'would you like to have a sandwich with me?'."

Butler, a declared republican, was appointed Governor of Tasmania from 3 October 2003. On 9 August 2004 he announced his resignation, saying he wanted to end a malicious campaign against him and his wife. His brief term was highly controversial and critics called him imperious and overbearing in office. His departure was not mourned.

One of the difficulties Mackay faced during his time in the job was that some ambassadors recalled the days of plenty when lavish embassies and residences were built. But by the early 1990s, Australia had been hit hard by a severe economic downturn, described by Treasurer Paul Keating as "the recession we had to have."

As with other departments, Administrative Services was expected to find savings and shortly beforehand it sold surplus land from the Australian embassy in Tokyo for $600 million. Mackay helped finance construction of the new embassy in Tokyo by selling its footpath for $90 million.

While the embassy in Beijing was being built, he was dispatched to meet the city's mayor to try to overcome a delay in having electricity connected. Not a diplomat by nature, he presented the mayor a gift of an album with a photograph showing the recently completed Chinese embassy in Canberra. The mayor wanted to know why the second half of the album was blank, and Mackay, in his finest diplomatic hour, replied that when the Australian embassy in Beijing was completed, photographs of it would round out the album.

But Chinese politics can be impenetrable to outsiders, and darker forces were at work. For reasons not known, though apparently in no way connected with Australia's embassy or Mackay's visit, the mayor was hanged several weeks later.

The appointment as general manager of the Overseas Property Group lasted only 14 months. Coming from an upbringing in the quiet backwater of Wellington, and meeting sons of presidents and mayors of foreign cities, and getting in to few dust-ups with ambassadors who wanted more than he could give left many memories that seem surreal. Some of the ambassadors remain good friends.

Those 14 months included at least seven overseas trips, including three around the world. Sometimes this brought the type of dislocation described by jetsetting entertainers who lose track of where on earth they are. John tried to ring home once and when the operator asked which city he was calling from, he was stumped. He scoured the room for a piece of hotel stationery and found out that way that he was in Manila.

Colette and John have done a great deal of private international travel— from brief trips to New Zealand to see the Brumbies or the Raiders to rewarding journeys in the USA, Europe, Africa, and the Mediterranean, where they cruised the Greek islands. With their great friends Allan and Janeen Williams and Ian and Darelle Carmody they've gone on four self drive barging holidays in the wine regions of France.

Pursuing their mutual interest in golf, the couple took a charter train and golf safari through South Africa, organised by their friends Richard and Maureen Tindale, who own the National Zoo and Aquarium in Canberra.

Their enjoyment of golf also took them to the USA, where the courses they played included Pebble Beach, California.

Eventually the senior executives of the Department decided the favours owed to Mackay had been repaid and he had had enough fun. So in June 1991 he was asked to be director of the Australian Protective Service—a job in which he had acted for about three months before working for West.

As head of the Service, he was responsible for about 1,000 staff spread around Australia. They included people highly trained in counter-terrorism, and most of Mackay's staff routinely wore guns. The atmosphere of the police or military was new to Mackay: "You would issue an order and people would say, 'Yes sir'. I had never encountered that at work or at home."

But with his recollection of Scouts and school cadets, the style of the service suited his personality. But he felt uncomfortable in the official uniform and only wore it when he had to.

The Service protected many major sites: residences of the Governor-General and the Prime Minister in Canberra and Sydney; embassies; Parliament House; the Lucas Heights nuclear reactor; and bases at Pine Gap, Woomera, Geraldton and Exmouth. It had trained counter-terrorist personnel at all major airports, and ran all the immigration detention centres on behalf of the Department of Immigration. This was to be another challenging and eventful assignment for John Mackay.

9

INTO THE HOT SEAT AT APS

Challenges came soon enough for the new head of the Australian Protective Service, the "APS". Early on the morning of 24 September 1991 there was the unwelcome news that an APS officer had accidentally fired his pistol in the basement of Parliament House. Correct procedure was to report this incident to the Parliament House security controller, Tony Curtis, but John Mackay decided not to.

As might have been expected, news of the episode eventually leaked.

"When it did come out several months later I had to do a great deal of tap dancing to explain our incompetence and secrecy."

Not much later, he planned an approved business trip and paid to include Colette, who so often took responsibility for the children while John was away. They made arrangements for care of the children and the dog, but all their plans were unravelled on 6 April 1992 by an attack by a gang of 15 men and women on the Iranian Embassy in Canberra.

At 2.44 a.m. that day the first wire service reports were received in Australia of attacks on Iranian embassies in Bonn, The Hague and London. Iranian Embassy staff in Canberra telephoned the APS ten minutes later, seeking protection following these reports and others from the embassy's own sources.

The APS duty officer immediately instructed the two nightshift mobile patrols to monitor all Iranian Embassy locations at least every 20 minutes and informed the embassy and the Australian Federal Police (AFP), which also included the embassy on its mobile patrols.

The frequency of patrols was later increased and a meeting between the AFP and the embassy was scheduled for 1 p.m. that day. The last of the patrols by the APS and AFP were at 11.40 a.m. and 11.45 a.m. Both noted no concern.

Shortly after noon an embassy car sought to leave the embassy compound. The car was set upon by the gang of attackers, who smashed its windows and dragged the chauffeur and another official from the car and began beating them. Other members of the gang rushed through the gates and entered the embassy building, damaged the chancery, set fire to furniture and cars, scrawled slogans on walls and assaulted staff. Two Iranian officials and an Australian chauffeur required hospital treatment after the attack, one with a depressed skull fracture.

At 12.07 p.m. embassy staff requested urgent assistance from the AFP. Police arrived at 12.13 p.m. and the APS at 12.15 p.m.

Unaware of the full significance of the embassy attack, Mackay dismissed his wife's concerns and continued to prepare for the overseas trip.

Next day, as they were preparing to board an aircraft in Sydney, one of Mackay's staff tapped him on the shoulder with the unwanted advice that his minister Nick Bolkus wanted to meet immediately in Canberra.

There was no choice but to cancel the overseas trip and attend the meeting in Canberra with various security agencies. The meeting ran through much of that night, trying to identify why there had been no security at the Iranian Embassy.

The mood of the meeting was that the APS was going to carry the blame. Then, at about 2 a.m., AFP Assistant Commissioner Bill Stoll beckoned Mackay and they left the room for a quick chat. He told Mackay that the AFP had received a telephone message from the APS suggesting that the Iranian embassy needed extra protection, but that Foreign Affairs had not agreed.

Another meeting was scheduled for about 8 a.m., before which Bolkus asked to see Mackay. Mackay recalls the minister's opening words: "Welcome back, Christopher Skase. What the fuck were you doing fleeing the country when we have this dreadful incident?"

At the time, Skase, with debts of more than $700 million, had recently fled to Majorca in Spain, where he lived for about 11 years until his death in August 2001. Bolkus had doubtless not intended the analogy literally, and it was of course unfair. Skase had left Australia to evade justice after being charged with improperly using his position to obtain management fees and apparently had no intention of returning. Mackay was leaving on official business with every intention of returning. But the decision to continue with the trip after the attack on the Embassy was a significant error of judgement.

For about 20 minutes Bolkus screamed at Mackay. After this ordeal, Mackay and his boss, acting Deputy Secretary Steve Palywoda were dismissed and ordered to wait, "I think so Bolkus could get his breath and give me another go."

Palywoda asked Mackay if he was alright. Assured by Mackay he was, Palywoda then asked what Mackay had been thinking about during this extraordinary dressing down. "I was thinking about that scene from the film, 'A Fish Called Wanda' where John Cleese was being held upside down outside the window and asked to apologise."

In the subsequent meeting before a panel of ministers, staff from Foreign Affairs were completely caught off guard, when Stoll was asked a pre-arranged question and disclosed the telephone record which confirmed where the blame lay for the failure to station security at the Embassy.

Under a user pays arrangement, the Department of Foreign Affairs paid the APS for its work. Though Foreign Affairs had received information which indicated a potential threat, it had not asked the APS to put anyone at the embassy. Australia and Iran were not close friends and to have requested protection would have cost the department money. Indeed, Foreign Affairs had only recently cut its security budget by $2 million despite protests by the APS.

An official inquiry headed by a former secretary of the Department of the Prime Minister and Cabinet, Michael Codd, highlighted a convoluted arrangement involving five government agencies or departments with responsibility for the security of diplomatic and consular missions. The inquiry found this arrangement was far too unwieldy, with evident weaknesses in the flow of intelligence from one agency to another. Codd found each agency had to bear some responsibility for the failure of security at the Iranian Embassy.

Mackay's error of judgement in heading overseas at such a time was in part caused by lack of knowledge about what was important in the early days of a new job. His judgement might also have been better had he not had such a long lunch with a colleague from the Department of Defence on the day of the attack on the embassy.

But his sense of humour remained. Several days later, while they were eating on an outside table at a Manuka restaurant, he told Colette they were supposed to be on a wharf in San Francisco eating seafood. At home, with a tap running, he reminded her they were supposed to be at Niagara Falls.

Despite the disappointment, Colette was gracious and simply returned to work, and they set about rounding up their children from various carers.

Mackay recovered quickly from the effects of his error, and humiliation by a government minister. "I'm not very good often at predicting the future. But when the future blows up in my face I am very good at recovering." He does not hold fond memories of Bolkus but recalls much later being greeted as a long-lost friend by his former minister in a small Canberra restaurant.

In a subsequent review of the APS, Mackay urged that it be removed from the Department of Administrative Services and its user pays system. The service was ultimately moved to the Attorney-General's Department, where Mackay found he had little in common with the phalanx of lawyers who seemed to think very little of the protective service.

He says the culture of the APS was pretty grubby at times, but the approach taken by some of the people who wrote anonymous complaints against him could be worse. Experienced at dealing with cranks, he was quite willing to toss their letters into a bin. But Attorney-General's was more likely to hold a major inquiry with the slightest provocation.

On one occasion, trying to find out who had written an anonymous complaint against him was a cause of regret. Mackay's inquiry failed to identify the writer but turned up "all this other shit I didn't really want to know about but which I had to deal with". Even worse was the queue of people at the door, wanting to know why he didn't trust them.

For all his devil may care attitude, John did take seriously a death threat against him from a former staffer whom he had sacked. The man was, after all, an explosives specialist, a gun enthusiast and a former corrupt cop.

Police alerted John to the threat, which they had learned about from the man's psychiatrist. John showed a photograph of the man to his children while they were watching television and told them about the danger. Ben, quite unconcerned, said to his sister Jane, "I think we are watching the wrong channel."

John concedes he was kept awake for a couple of weeks, but nothing came of the threat. After several weeks the family became tired of the constant intrusion of police car flashing lights through the house windows and requested that the security cease.

As the manager of Australia's immigration detention centres, the APS arrange some deportations. On his way to Sydney for a regional commanders' conference, on 4 November 1992, Mackay was telephoned by a deputy secretary of the Department of Immigration, Mark Sullivan, and requested to arrange deportation of 113 Chinese nationals from Christmas Island. They had arrived by boat on 30 October. Their applications for residency were refused and the Government decided to send them home.

The conference was changed to a planning operation which had 36 hours to arrange an aircraft and 52 physically strong staff to accompany the deportees to China. As the exercise was being planned, the finance manager, Lin Stock, revealed she was fluent in Mandarin, so she was included in the team to fly to China.

The department chartered a Qantas plane and held a training exercise en route from Sydney to Christmas Island on Saturday 7 November. The Chinese were not told of their destination until they had arrived at the airport and were about to board the aircraft. After a change of aircraft crew in Singapore, the flight landed in Guangzhou where they were transferred to Chinese authorities.

Having learned from his experience of the Iranian Embassy fiasco, Mackay stayed in Australia to deal with media inquiries, and missed the reportedly spectacular party aboard on the return flight to Sydney after the assignment had been completed. Worse still, this dutiful sacrifice was in vain—there were almost no media inquiries.

The media did pay attention to an incident from 3 to 5 August 1992, when inmates climbed onto the roof of the Port Hedland Detention Centre and threatened to jump. They were protesting against the rejection of their appeals for refugee status. From distant Canberra, Mackay tried to find some way of preventing anyone getting hurt when they jumped. Several did jump, sustained spinal injuries and were taken to hospital in Perth.

"It was just like a hostage situation." After the first person jumped, he considered whether to have the building stormed to bring the people down, but it would have risked injury to them and to APS's staff.

Immigration minister Gerry Hand met with Mark Sullivan and Mackay well into the night and they finally arranged for the Minister to fly to Port Hedland in a VIP jet. In years to come circumstances were to draw Sullivan and Mackay together again, to face more complicated challenges.

Hand made it clear that if people were still on the roof when the plane landed in Brisbane, he would not continue to Port Hedland. By then several had jumped and been seriously injured. Hand did not continue to Port Hedland and it was up to APS staff to negotiate with those still on the roof to come down. "Whilst the setting up and running of detention centres was very interesting from a practical point of view, I always felt desperately sorry for these people and still do," Mackay said.

One of the early security breaches at Australia's new Parliament House, opened by the Queen on 9 May 1988, occurred on 12 August 1992, when Clifton Moss, of Broken Hill, apparently with a complaint against the South Australian Government, drove his Mitsubishi Pajero through the front doors of Parliament House in Canberra and into the Great Hall. This was only four months after the attack on the Iranian Embassy.

A subsequent review of security recommended bollards be constructed between the columns under the front veranda to prevent vehicles being driven through the front doors. Undaunted, in 1994, Moss drove his vehicle into the ceremonial pond and in 1996 threw a brick into security equipment at the main entrance. This resulted in a restraining order against him which had the desired effect. However, he was later arrested elsewhere for damaging public buildings.

Mackay was conscious the APS had attracted some blame for the Pajero incident, but he also knew there was considerable ill will between the APS and the AFP. Parliament House security superintendent Tony Curtis, seconded for two years from the AFP, did not want the APS in the building. This view was shared by the Speaker of the House of Representatives, Leo McCleay, who wanted the APS replaced by the AFP. At least one of the reasons for this was the fee for service charged by the APS as part of the Department of Administrative Services.

McLeay summoned Mackay to Sydney and demanded, among other things, to know why, in the Pajero incident, Mackay's staff had not shot out the tires of the vehicle, or indeed why they had not shot the driver. But officially, the APS recognised it would have been difficult for the officer stationed near the front door to have stopped the vehicle without injuring himself or visitors. And decades later, the APS continues to provide security at Parliament House.

The Pajero incident highlighted the anomalous nature of security arrangements at Parliament House. Although the APS had responsibility for controlling the Pajero for the few seconds it sped up the forecourt towards the main entrance, once through the front doors the vehicle became the responsibility of Parliament House security staff. But they were not trained to apprehend an armed man, nor to identify potential explosives. And once the vehicle was inside, APS officers were not authorised to deal with the situation.

Meanwhile, for reasons not entirely clear, a telephone call to the APS from Judy Lynne, of Balloon Aloft, was put through to the head of the service. Balloon Aloft was running a festival in Canberra in 1993. The call that John answered was destined to lead to a marked change in his understanding of the leadership role.

Judy Lynne wanted APS sponsorship to bring a hot air balloon from Canada that could accommodate a wheelchair.

Funds raised from the balloon festival, one of the first to be held in Canberra, were to assist Camp Quality, which supports young people who have cancer. The difficulty was there was no balloon in Australia that could accommodate many of those young people.

Without hesitation, Mackay agreed to the $3,000 sponsorship and the balloon duly arrived. Its first passenger was a young man of about 18, whose disability had confined him for some years to an aged person's home in northern New South Wales. After the exhilarating experience of riding in the balloon, he read some poetry and the reading was televised around Australia. Not surprisingly, this evoked considerable emotion, not least in John Mackay.

During the festival John accepted an invitation to ride in a balloon flown by a world champion. The craft did not have a traditional basket but two seats. After a safe landing he insisted his daughter, Claire, also have a ride, which she did.

At the conclusion of the festival Mackay was invited to the stage, presented with a small gift and thanked for the sponsorship so generously provided by the APS. Already unsure whether this donation would attract criticism when he faced Senate estimates, Mackay declared that in future it would not be necessary to bring a balloon from Canada to accommodate wheelchairs. "I am going to buy you one."

This spontaneous declaration was made with no knowledge of the financial commitment involved. So he walked over to Judy Lynne who told him the cost was about $50,000 and left him to ponder how to fulfil his promise. One thing was certain—a $3,000 sponsorship might get through, but $50,000 for the APS to buy a balloon would never pass the scrutiny of the Senate Estimates Committee.

Coincidentally, planning was underway for a team building exercise of APS staff from around Australia. Two groups of about 50 met in Bowral New South Wales. As part of that meeting, Mackay showed a video of the young man in his wheelchair having his ride in the hot air balloon. He then challenged staff to cash in and donate unused leave to buy a balloon which could accommodate a wheelchair. "Everybody got behind this balloon and we raised the money in no time. People donated weeks of leave. They all had more leave than they knew what to do with and this was a soft, easy way of putting a lot of money together."

Mackay arranged for the ACT region of the APS to buy a trailer, ostensibly to take targets to the firing range. The trailer's design suited it also to transporting a hot air balloon.

The balloon duly arrived from England displaying the APS logo and with a basket that could carry a wheelchair and ensure the passenger a good view. "This was a tremendous way of inspiring the APS—that we were doing something really special for the community. Even externally it raised our profile quite a lot."

The balloon was taken around Australia for many years, mostly with children supported by Camp Quality as passengers.

Camp Quality Australia was established in 1983 to provide children living with cancer and their families with a support network. Its first camp was held at Vision Valley in New South Wales.

APS staff frequently asked John how their balloon was going as he travelled around. "This was probably the first time I realised a leader can use his power and influence to achieve additional good things beyond the direct remit of his position. And he can inspire his organisation at the same time." He later used a similar strategy to raise money for the Salvation Army's Red Shield Appeal.

Relieved that the sponsorship of the balloon had escaped scrutiny by the Senate Estimates Committee, Mackay still had to wonder whether two other large expenditures would similarly be spared.

The Bowral team building exercise itself was one. The exercise was his idea, but he entrusted its organisation to others. They chose Milton Park Country House Hotel, which advertised "luxurious accommodation, fine cuisine and impeccable service in an atmosphere of relaxed sophistication." Conference participants enjoyed fabulous meals, including a grand dinner where a few people ordered expensive drinks and even cigars.

"I didn't take much notice because I was more focused on the people feeling like they were important; teaching them some new values, and making them work more like a team. This all worked amazingly well and the feedback was fantastic. It was not until some weeks later that I saw the bill! It was outrageously expensive and itemised the cigars and expensive drinks. It made me feel ill. I knew I would be in big trouble if anyone ever asked about it. Fortunately they never did."

Time came for the move of the APS headquarters to West Block, then a tired, sub-standard office building in the Parliamentary Triangle. One of the earliest government buildings in Canberra, it was a defined bomb shelter during World War Two and accommodated international communications during the war.

As seemed reasonable, Mackay arranged for the wing of the building into which the APS moved to be refurbished and refurnished in its former glory. "This instruction was carried out to the letter and I was a bit taken aback when I saw how well it had been done with lots of beautiful timber walls and very high ornate ceilings. There was even a very special handmade meeting table in the main conference room."

At about the same time Prime Minister Keating, with a known penchant for fine furniture, had had a new handmade dining table installed at the Lodge. Having preached the need for financial constraint, Keating drew considerable criticism when the cost of the table, about $20,000, was made public.

The new table in the APS conference room had cost at least that much and Mackay anticipated he would face similar criticism if the cost were made public. "Again, no-one ever asked."

10

THE RAIDERS—
A LABOUR OF LOVE

The coach of the Canberra Raiders Rugby League team, Tim Sheens, telephoned in 1993 to ask whether John could find a job in the Australian Protective Service for an up and coming player. At the time, David Furner was working in a hardware shop and finding it difficult to meet the demands of his job and his commitment to the Raiders.

Furner's father Don was a former Raiders coach, a role his son would later take up. Sheens said David was going to be a really great player.

"Loving the Raiders, I instantly thought this was a fantastic idea." So Furner was invited to an interview where he was offered a job as a protective service officer, despite not having done the basic training. The offer included an assurance that he would be allowed off work when he had to attend training.

But perhaps reasonably, the Community and Public Sector Union said it was improper for anyone to be appointed without the normal merit process and without basic training. "The union went absolutely ape-shit." The row attracted a lot of media coverage and typically, John was left looking for a Mackay solution so he could honour his promise.

With a mate who ran a recruiting business he worked out a contrived arrangement over the phone. The recruiting business hired Furner and Mackay took him on as a consultant in the administration section, which looked after such matters as payroll and purchasing.

Celebrating the triumph of the Canberra Raiders Rugby League team with Mal Meninga, after the grand final win in 1989.

"He was an absolute hit." By chance, Furner worked beside Andrew Bishop, then an Aussie rules player and much later the kicking coach for the Raiders. The two got on well and David Furner repaid John's faith in him by working extremely hard.

"I would see him on a Sunday afternoon get the daylights belted out of him at Canberra Stadium. He would be the first in the office the next morning. He had a fantastic work attitude. Everybody loved him and he worked really, really well."

Furner was soon playing first grade for the Raiders and within 12 months scored the first try in the 1994 grand final in which the Raiders beat Canterbury 36–12. The result was a fitting send-off for the Raiders' retiring captain Mal Meninga. Furner won the Clive Churchill Medal and was selected in the Kangaroo tour of Great Britain and France a few days later.

Clearly, Sheens's early judgement of Furner proved correct and Mackay is willing to claim his share of the credit for the player's success. After that winning grand final, John possibly jeopardised Furner's trip to England by accompanying him on a night out in Canberra only a day or so before the team was due to depart. Though there was some drinking, the night ended on a most positive note. At the Canberra Workers Club, David Furner was recognised by a group of intellectually disabled people, one of whom Mackay had recruited and who worked beside Furner. The entire group was delighted when the rugby league star spent some time with them.

Being with footballers at close quarters impressed John Mackay with the rock star status they were accorded after the big win. He recalls too their generous response when asked to sign autographs by the many people who recognised them. "They always had time to say something nice and to sign something."

Furner remained at the APS for several years. Insisting that he should not have to take leave when he represented Australia with the Kangaroos got Mackay into some hot water with the auditors. "I just told them to go to buggery and we moved on."

The two men became close friends. Indeed, John went to Furner's wedding, and before that to his bucks' party, which took the form of a golf game with a different hotel representing each hole. The first hotel was a par 3, which meant the players drank three schooners. John reckons he lasted only about four holes.

Later unfortunately, as a member of the board of the Canberra Raiders, Mackay, who had played such an important role in Furner's early career, also had a hand in his dismissal as coach of the team they loved.

In 2009, not many years after David Furner's playing career ended, the Raiders appointed him coach. As the son of the club's first coach, Don Furner senior, and the brother of the chief executive, Don junior, he immediately attracted accusations of nepotism. But generally his appointment was welcomed. The Raiders had made the finals in 2008 and it seemed David had inherited a team that would do well.

It did not. Furner's first season as coach began with the loss of seven of the first nine games and the team finished the year 13th. This continued a pattern of making the finals, only to miss out in subsequent years.

The Raiders made the finals in 2010 and Furner's four year contract was extended for another two years. About halfway through the 2011 season, with the Raiders effectively replicating the 2009 season, the extension of his contract was widely criticised and his future was in doubt. John Mackay, who had joined the Raiders' board in 2004, said publicly that Furner would have to lose another 30 games before his position was questioned.

The Raiders made the finals in 2012 but 2013 began badly. Success on the field was initially reasonable, but in a widely publicised act of stupidity, team member Josh Dugan photographed himself sitting and drinking on the roof of his house when he was supposed to be recovering from an injury. Dugan's contract with the Raiders was terminated on 14 March and on 10 May he signed a contract with St George Illawarra for the remainder of the season.

There was further off field drama when another player, Blake Ferguson, was seen frequently drunk, sometimes with Dugan in Sydney, while undergoing rehabilitation from an injury. He too was subsequently sacked.

On field performance deteriorated and it was clear the team would not make the finals. But on 20 August 2013, when the board met and unanimously voted to terminate Furner's contract, even those close to the club were shocked. The task of telling the coach of his dismissal fell to his brother, Don, as CEO. Don drove to a Raiders team camp on the south coast to deliver an immediate termination notice to his brother.

The board's decision came about seven weeks after an assurance by club chairman John McIntyre that Furner's position was safe. The team was then in 11th place on the league table. When the board decided to sack Furner, the Raiders were in ninth place and had a slight chance of making the finals. So why was the coach sacked three weeks before the end of the home and away season?

On 2 August the sports editor of *The Canberra Times*, Chris Wilson, wrote that player power had contributed. Wilson said senior players had grown frustrated at the leniency shown to misbehaving stars such as Dugan and Ferguson, who had made the 2013 campaign a disaster.

Speaking some weeks after Furner's sacking, Mackay said several board members had been uncomfortable with the team's 2012 performance. They felt that the coach had good players who were not performing well and the players seemed to have more injuries than was reasonable. "I was of a mind to recommend that he be sacked at the end of the [2012] season."

Over lunch with David, John let him know there was a move to sack him. "Being a mate of his, I felt compelled to tell him I would be supporting it if such a move was on."

Later, with chairman McIntyre absent, at least two board meetings discussed terminating Furner's contract. On his return, McIntyre did not support the move and, largely out of respect for McIntyre, the board agreed Furner would stay. That decision took into consideration that Furner's wife was undergoing treatment for breast cancer.

John describes 2013 as yet another horror year. The loss of Dugan and Ferguson, players with immense talent, was symptomatic of the coach having lost control of the players. "We had those players because the coach wanted them and as it turned out for whatever reason he was unable to get the best out of them on a consistent basis. Both were chewing up an enormous amount of salary cap."

They were also occupying a lot of management time while earning the Raiders much public criticism. Many supporters were fed up with the adverse publicity. Supporters were reminded of the dismissal in 2008, before Furner's appointment as coach, of Todd Carney. Like Dugan and Ferguson, Carney had exceptional ability as a rugby league player but the Raiders, and the National Rugby League, finally lost patience with his repeated alcohol related misdemeanours, which went close to earning him a prison sentence. He was deregistered by the NRL until 2010, when he joined the Sydney Roosters. By mid-2011, Carney's continued off field misbehaviour became widely known and his contract with the Roosters was terminated in September. Despite his record, and because of his playing brilliance, he was promptly signed by the Cronulla Sharks. The Sharks sacked him in 2014 after a photo of him engaging in a vulgar act circulated on social media.

The pattern of delinquent player behaviour no doubt influenced the Raiders' board to look to a new beginning. The board decided it had to remove Furner before the end of the season. Delay could mean the loss of other good players and of the opportunity to recruit the best available replacement coach.

John says the decision, made more in sadness than anger, recognised the players had simply stopped listening to the coach. Furner was well compensated and several board members met with him subsequently.

The board's decision to replace him with Ricky Stuart, also a former Raiders player, was not universally welcome. Critics observed that Stuart's coaching record at three previous clubs was worse than Furner's had been at the Raiders. But for John, Stuart had proved himself as coach of the New South Wales State of Origin team, when he went so close to breaking the Queensland stranglehold. "We didn't take very long to realise Ricky would be the ideal replacement, despite the fact we had half a dozen applicants who could do the job." In 2014, Stuart's first year as coach, the Raiders finished second last.

Of course the relationship with David Furner over some 20 years is only a part of John Mackay's role on the Raiders board. Directors are responsible to sponsors and fans as well as for success on the field.

11

DISSENT, DANGER AND DOGGY-DOO

Shortly before the 1994 federal budget, Mackay's departmental secretary John Mellors telephoned late at night to ask how much it would cost to insulate thousands of houses under the flight path to the north of Sydney Airport. There was pressure to include a figure that night in the budget, and Mellors believed Mackay's guess would be better than his. So Mackay suggested $60 million should give some latitude.

The noise insulation program, largely prompted by a political desire to retain seats under the flight path of a third runway at Sydney Airport, was subsequently announced and Mackay was largely responsible for administering it. It ultimately cost $600 million.

While it was underway, the cost would become a relatively minor concern for John Mackay. Over the 1994/95 year he travelled once or twice each week to Sydney to negotiate the sealing of houses, schools, churches and other buildings against aircraft noise. Properties, once sealed, had to be air conditioned. The cost for each house reached $40,000 to $50,000.

Disputes began with people who were not eligible because they lived just outside the program's boundary. Then Marrickville Council became involved over what it saw as shortcomings of the program or inadequate work. There was also concern over the demolition of more than 100 houses in Sydenham, one of Sydney's oldest suburbs.

Mackay, as a bureaucrat from Canberra, was subjected to personal abuse and more. At one meeting, someone threw coffee over him; on leaving another he found his car smeared with dog droppings. During a rowdy meeting at Marrickville Town Hall while trying to explain the program and answer questions, he became concerned for his safety. He could see only one exit and to reach it he had to pass through the angry mob.

On another occasion his Minister Frank Walker, Transport Minister Laurie Brereton, and John Mackay went to a meeting at the Newtown Leagues Club.

Mackay had assured both ministers that he had the situation pretty much under control, but the volatile crowd was anything but under control. Doors at the club were smashed and the ministers were jostled and sought sanctuary in Commonwealth cars at the back of the building. To make it worse Brereton had one of his children with him. On their return to Canberra that afternoon in the Prime Minister's VIP jet, Mackay remained a discreet distance from both ministers.

It was one of those programs in which he found it difficult to take a trick. In an attempt to counter the adverse publicity that plagued it, he briefed a *Sydney Morning Herald* journalist on the merits and achievements of the scheme. Buoyed by the seemingly reasonable attitude of this journalist, his sensible questions and accurate note taking, Mackay sent a message to Walker that this decent journalist would ensure that the scheme had a good run in the next day's *Herald*. "I was nearly violently ill when I read the story. It was worse than anything I had ever seen."

The psychological bruising he received and the physical scars he could easily have suffered while administering the program came with an out front management style which meant criticism would naturally be directed at him. He learned much about implementing huge programs that affected many people's lives and remained philosophical about the personal cost.

This type of hands on involvement was not typical of many bureaucrats, but quite normal in John Mackay's work outside the federal public service.

After the Australian Protective Service was transferred to the Attorney-General's Department, Mackay, somewhat to his surprise, was promoted to band 2 in the Senior Executive Service (SES). "I was like a fish out of water in A-G's. I had absolutely nothing in common with about 90 per cent of the department." He did have a close relationship with the staff involved in national security, but it came as something of a relief to be telephoned by former boss, John Mellors, and encouraged to apply for a deputy secretary's job coming up in the Department of Administrative Services.

"I think he admired me in some ways but not in all ways. But he saw I could balance his senior management team with my approach. He had some other weird characters, including himself. John was just an absolute flat earth economist in many ways. He and I had had some dreadful brawls at various stages."

"I couldn't get out of A-G's fast enough. And being incredibly ambitious all my life, I couldn't wait to get my hands on a deputy secretary's job which was so far beyond anything I had ever dreamt of."

Getting the job was great, but it soon turned out he had inherited a department which was about to be eviscerated. The Keating government had recognised that much of the work then being done by the Department of Administrative Services could be done more effectively by the private sector.

Under its minister, Frank Walker, Mackay settled in well to the Department, not least because it was a can-do department with little emphasis on policy. "My jobs were all in various ways operational rather than policy based."

The department had two other deputy secretaries. All three were markedly different in style, but despite the differences, the team worked effectively if not harmoniously. Meanwhile, Mellors had been asked to produce a cabinet submission on the future of the Department. In particular, whether functions would continue to be done within government or should be outsourced to the private sector.

Mackay found Mellors to be intense, and bright academically. Mellors might go home, drink some wine, play his guitar until about 2 a.m., then write a brilliant paper. Both men were smokers and enjoyed a drink. Though they were very different personalities, Mackay admired Mellors, "particularly because he was so much brighter than I was."

At first there were about ten business units reporting to Mackay, operating on principles established by Mellors. It was clear that most of these could not continue as they were. They included the staff managing the Commonwealth vehicle fleet, warehousing and distribution, major construction, building maintenance, interior design, and environmental services. Printing, interior design and other business units were being run by public servants. In the mid-1990s, state and federal governments were increasingly applying competitive principles to many of their operations.

A major player in the development of the National Competition Policy was Gary Sturgess. In March 1983 he joined the staff of the newly elected Leader of the New South Wales Opposition, Nick Greiner, as the director of Research and Policy Development.

Sturgess also directed extensive research into official corruption in the New South Wales Government, contributing to public inquiries and criminal prosecutions. But it was as a competition guru that Mackay engaged Sturgess to advise on a major restructure of the business units of the Department of Administrative Services. His advice would ultimately lead to their privatisation.

Mackay met Sturgess at Canberra Airport and as they drove to the office they spoke of the redundant functions still prevalent in many public service departments. To Mackay's great embarrassment, as the two left a lift to walk to Mackay's office, they were greeted by the tea lady.

Sturgess applied what he called "the Yellow Pages test" to determine whether particular business units should continue. The test was simply that if any function performed by the department could be found in the Yellow Pages, there was no basis for its being done by government.

The entire House of Representatives roared with laughter the day the Minister for Administrative Services, David Jull, attempted to say the business units were being reformed according to the "Hilmer Principles" devised by management professor Fred Hilmer. Instead, Jull said the units were being reformed according to the "Himmler Principles". Some people have mused since that Jull's Freudian slip might have been closer to the mark than he realised.

For the next two years or so, Mackay led the privatisation of eight of the ten businesses reporting to him. He began with the principle that those who had to lose their jobs should at least leave with smiles on their faces and their dignity intact.

Fleet, effectively a government-run car leasing business, was sold to Macquarie Bank for about $300 million. Though it was important for sales such as this to realise a good return for the government, Mackay was prepared to sacrifice the last dollar if that meant ensuring fair treatment of the people who would continue to work in that business. Three of the eight businesses sold were bought by the staff who worked in them. These were marginal businesses while run by the government but became profitable after their sale. Interiors Australia continues to operate in Canberra almost 20 years later.

The sale of the eight businesses, involving about 4000 staff, realised about $800 million. Mackay was left with only 200 staff reporting to him.

While arranging to sell the eight businesses, Mackay was also responsible for Commonwealth property. Under the Howard government there was strong pressure to sell numerous Commonwealth buildings. Mackay worked closely with the Minister, David Jull. They got on well, perhaps because both were then heavy smokers.

Jull was a lovely man, John says. They travelled around Asia to drum up interest in the properties that the government no longer wanted. The trip suited Jull who was interested in aviation and in Thai food, interests Mackay was happy to share.

At the old Hong Kong airport, Mackay looked at Jull watching the takeoffs and landings. Pilots needed considerable skill to land at that most difficult airport and he suggested to Jull they spend some time watching the approaching aircraft line up on the chequer board pattern displayed on a huge billboard on a nearby hillside. Jull watched in awe as huge jumbo jets, at one moment heading straight for them, made delicate manoeuvres to land safely. It was difficult to get Jull to leave. The two men became good friends and stayed in touch. David Jull died in 2011.

Mackay described himself as left leaning but held strongly to the view that whoever was elected would have his full support. "I have gone very close to being sacked by both sides, which I am very proud of. I think that is a badge of honour."

A major scandal erupted over ministerial allowances while Mackay was still at the Department of Administrative Services. There were several sackings and Jull resigned from the ministry following accusations that he had failed to prevent other politicians from abusing their parliamentary allowances. Mackay had no involvement in the matter but with only a couple of hundred staff remaining and the department in a shambles, he realised the time for his departure was rapidly approaching.

Having first shown his plan of how to abolish the department to Mellors, who effectively approved it, Mackay went to the Department of Prime Minister and Cabinet with the plan. It was accepted and very shortly after, most of what was left of the department was incorporated into the Department of Finance and Administration. The remainder went to the Department of Prime Minister and Cabinet.

Shortly before this occurred, the head of Finance and Administration, Peter Boxall, rang to say he was on his way to speak about Mackay's future in the merged department. On his way he would speak to Mackay's colleague, Brendan Godfrey.

It was surprising when Boxall turned up in Mackay's office only about ten minutes later. Had Godfrey not been in? Yes, he had been in, said Boxall. Mackay then realised Godfrey had been sacked.

The conversation with Mackay took a little longer. First, Boxall said he would like Mackay to remain in Boxall's department. Mackay was pleased but informed Boxall he had applied for two jobs and, not choosing to hide his light under a bushel, said he expected to be offered both jobs. As it happened, he was.

Somewhat magnanimously, Mackay offered to stay on to help integrate what was left of the Department of Administrative Services with Finance and Administration. This offer was accepted though Mackay was told he would not be a deputy secretary, only a general manager.

Mackay responded he had worked hard to become a deputy secretary and that unless he went as a deputy secretary he would not go at all. Boxall retreated to another room for a brief discussion with his deputy secretary, Len Early, and returned to tell Mackay he also would be a deputy secretary.

Mackay remained in the new position for only about eight weeks, during which he had to appear before a Senate Estimates Committee. There he faced the formidable and frequently caustic Labor senators, Robert Ray and John Faulkner. Both, it seems, had been well armed with information provided by one of Mackay's former peers. The senators asked for details about the operation of a mini-bar in Mackay's office. He responded that it was really quite simple. "When it is empty I get someone to fill it up again."

Fortunately, this amused the good senators, and there were no further questions. However, Mackay received a message from Boxall instructing him to shut up. "I didn't think much of Boxall and I don't think he thought much of me."

Boxall's opinion would not have been enhanced by Mackay's appearance and demeanour at a division heads meeting the morning after his farewell from Administrative Services, held at the Canberra Casino. John left about 4 a.m. and Colette had to drive him to the 8 a.m. meeting.

"I'm sure they were not the slightest bit amused with my appearance or aroma."

When it was obviously time to leave Administrative Services, John sought advice from friend and former work colleague, Ian Hansen. With Hansen's encouragement, he applied for the position of chief executive officer of ACT Electricity and Water (ACTEW). He also applied to be head of the Australian Maritime Safety Authority. The latter position, with three ships sailing around Australia's coastline and the opportunity for something like a boy's own adventure, particularly appealed. Its focus was practical—something like the Australian Protective Service.

He was offered both jobs and was undecided which to accept. Allan Hawke, who had become a lifelong friend, strongly recommended Mackay to the chair of ACTEW, Jim Service. John was still thinking of becoming a department secretary, but Hawke suggested to him it was time to move out of his comfort zone of the public service. Finally he accepted the ACTEW job, after interviews with the ACTEW board and the board of the Australian Maritime Safety Authority.

The decision was neither easy nor clear cut. He knew the Maritime Safety Authority really wanted him too.

"I was obviously far better than anybody else they had in mind. I remember them trying to convince me to change my mind when I finally told them I was going to go to ACTEW."

12

ON THE HIGH WIRE
AT ACTEW

ccepting the job at ACTEW felt like a much bigger risk. "I was stepping a long way further outside my comfort zone. AMSA would have been a bit like running the Australian Protective Service, which I could have done with one hand tied behind my back."

But the ACTEW job meant working for a new government in a public utility. John had the basic skills for the job but he would be more like a one man band, effectively working to a private board. "That might have been a bit more of a risk."

In 1988, when the ACT Electricity Authority assumed responsibility for the ACT's water supply, ACTEW was born. It became a territory owned corporation and the ACT Government's most lucrative business. ACTEW's future was of particular concern to the ACT's Chief Minister, Kate Carnell, who was not consulted over the Mackay appointment. Indeed, she had expressed some concern about it at first.

Mackay's appointment as chief executive officer was announced on 19 December 1997. It was the first the author had heard of John Mackay but the day marked the beginning of numerous interviews and discussions from which a high level of trust and respect developed.

Perhaps indicating that he knew less about his new job than he might have, Mackay told *The Canberra Times* on 20 December 1997 it would be an absolute crying shame if ACTEW had to merge with another organisation.

In his ActewAGL office in 2004.

"Certainly while I have any strength left in me ACTEW will survive and prosper."

He said there were real challenges to provide high quality, cost efficient and reliable services. His initial challenge was to maintain the standards and to seek opportunities to improve them. Competition from other electricity suppliers would be the major challenge down the track. But he had no doubt ACTEW could survive in its own right. "The people of the ACT have a direct interest in making sure that occurs."

Many years later, John said the thought of selling or merging ACTEW was more in the minds of its board and the ACT Government than in his. But clearly it was recognised that he had a background in privatising businesses. Other utilities, particularly in Victoria, were being privatised, but this possibility was not raised in the first discussion with Jim Service.

Goals which were set for Mackay at that first meeting included the establishment of a telecommunications business, TransACT, and the commercialisation of a sewage treatment system, CRANOS. Although there was no talk then of privatisation, the future of ACTEW, including its sale, became a very public subject of discussion soon after Mackay assumed his new position.

John Mackay formally began as ACTEW CEO on 27 January 1998. Within a few days he found division among the management team. Some had applied for the CEO position and had continued brawling among themselves. It did not take Mackay long to realise that significant changes were required, and not just to deal with disputes between managers. ACTEW, with a strong engineering tradition, had a workshop with 19 mechanics servicing motor vehicles. In his first day on the job, Mackay decided the workshop and its staff would have to go. This was only the first step in his plan to make the corporation more efficient. Within the next 12 months he initiated several hundred retrenchments. He also had to manage some public disquiet over two major billing failures within the first couple of months of his appointment.

ACTEW staff then occupied all ten office floors of Electricity House in London Circuit and four floors in other buildings. After the redundancy program which Mackay instigated, ACTEW rented no floors in other buildings and let four floors in Electricity House. "It just needed a huge cleanout." He sold the vehicle fleet and the property that had housed the workshop. After all the changes, he said, "I don't think anybody noticed the difference."

If the public did not notice that difference, the same cannot be said of Chief Minister Carnell's decision to sell ACTEW.

Though there was already some uncertainty over the future of ACTEW, it was not a major issue during the election campaign for the ACT Legislative Assembly. The election was on 21 February 1998, and Carnell's return to government was confirmed at the first sitting of the Assembly on 19 March 1998, when she secured the support of sufficient independents.

Soon after her return as Chief Minister, concerned over competition in the electricity market and with a desire for money to fund the government's superannuation liability, Carnell sought to sell ACTEW. She led a minority government and the proposal to sell was defeated in the Assembly. The six Labor members, the sole Greens member and three independents opposed the government. But the further development of national competition policy and the fact that ACTEW was one of Australia's smallest utilities convinced the government, the board and Mackay that it could not survive as it was.

On 9 April 1999, Carnell announced a study to examine the viability of merging ACTEW's operations with those of Great Southern Energy, then the electricity utility in southern New South Wales. On the following day the ACT Government advertised nationally for expressions of interest from other utilities interested in a partnership with ACTEW.

That is why AGL's Ian Woodward telephoned Mackay with the basis of an idea. Like Mackay, Woodward recognised that ACTEW would not merge with Great Southern Energy and that there was little likelihood of a private sale.

"So I sat down with Woodward for not all that long and I thought his proposal was bloody brilliant." The proposal was to merge AGL's gas business in the ACT with ACTEW's electricity business.

"Their gas business was not worth as much as our electricity business so the government would get a big cheque. We would have a much more powerful utility because we would cover gas and electricity. And the water business would remain effectively in government hands, albeit contracted out to this new thing called ActewAGL to manage."

The proposal was welcomed by some if not all ACTEW board members, who were concerned about their responsibilities as directors of the corporation. Several board members resigned, but Mackay, ever an optimist, and drawing on his experience and contacts from his work in the Department of Administrative Services, was thriving. "We basically knocked out a deal that people could wear. It was not all plain sailing."

In a telephone call the merchant banker advising ACTEW told of a rather technical financial requirement of AGL's. Mackay gave some frank advice to the caller: "I said 'I want you to hop up from the table, put your papers in your bag, tell them all to get fucked and walk out.' He said, 'Sorry John, I should have mentioned you're on loudspeaker.' So I said, 'Then you won't need to tell them anything. Put your papers in your bag and come home'."

But the deal did not collapse; AGL decided to approach the matter from a different angle.

On another occasion in the multi-million negotiations, a dispute arose over about $200,000. "Finally I said to the AGL bloke, I'll toss you for it."

A compromise was achieved and the deal was settled, though it still required approval by the ACT Legislative Assembly.

Late in 1999 Mackay unintentionally sent a confidential email to the author, who was then a journalist with *The Canberra Times*. The email was meant for David Graham, on the staff of ACTEW, but the sender accidentally selected Graham Downie as the recipient.

Mackay's message said something like "Mate, let me know what you think of this." The attachment to the email was not included, but it was clear from the message that negotiations between ACTEW and AGL were well advanced. He can see the funny side now, but when I telephoned, Mackay was at first confused, then horrified when he realised he had sent me the confidential email.

"Oh Christ, oh shit, fuck mate, what do you drink?" asked the distraught CEO. I responded that I drank water, of which ACTEW had plenty.

It was quite obvious that negotiations with AGL were at a delicate stage and premature reporting of the matter could cause the proposed venture to collapse. So we came to an agreement that I would hold back on my scoop, but *The Canberra Times* would be the first media outlet with the story if the deal was settled. So it was that an exclusive briefing was given from Carnell's office in early December 1999 and details of the proposed joint venture were published the next day.

AGL supplied gas to many Australian customers. If ACTEW could team up with AGL, the new entity would be Australia's first utility to provide electricity, gas, water and sewerage services.

About two weeks later, ACTEW's board chair Jim Service said a due diligence study would be held before the board could formally recommend a joint venture with AGL to the government. But of the 29 proposals received, that by AGL had been the only one worth pursuing.

On 29 February 2000, with the future of the utility being debated almost daily, Mackay declared publicly that ACTEW would simply become an electricity wholesaler and would wither on the vine if the joint venture with AGL did not go ahead. Seeking to persuade ACT Legislative Assembly members to support the deal, he said the Assembly had already ruled out the sale of ACTEW and a merger with another government-owned utility. If it ruled out the joint venture with a responsible Australian company which already had considerable assets in the ACT, there was only one other possibility on the agenda and ACTEW would have to play the cards dealt to it by the Assembly. Some Assembly members said that all ACTEW needed to do was to get out of retail electricity. But this would move ACTEW to a position where it had no chance of growth and so would start to wither on the vine.

If the Assembly could not support a joint venture with Australia's second oldest company, there would be absolutely no hope of its agreeing to a joint venture with an overseas company that had no connection with Canberra. Neither was it likely that another company, at least in the short term, would seek to convince the Assembly, Mackay said, "because they would know they had no chance."

On the same day, AGL managing director Len Bleasel advised the Australian Stock Exchange of a series of regional development initiatives planned for the ACT, if the proposed joint venture proceeded. The initiatives included the development, management and operation of a 90 megawatt gas-fired power generation plant in the ACT; the development of a separate ACT call centre that would be integrated into AGL's national call centre system; and the establishment of the national headquarters of an AGL infrastructure management and services business in the ACT.

ARTISTS IMPRESSION OF THE
REVISED POWER PLANT:

ACTEW

BACK PEDALLING

Canberra Times cartoonist Pope's view of ACTEW's revised position on the planned gas-fired power generator.

AGL's group general manager of corporate development, Ian Woodward, said that apart from the economic benefits to the ACT of the joint venture, the proposed gas-fired generator would initially provide about 30 per cent of the territory's electricity needs, with an option to expand. Initial estimates showed that the generator would contribute 15 to 20 per cent of the ACT's required greenhouse emissions reduction target.

Fourteen years later, the generator has not been built. A similar project was first proposed in 1995 by Mackay's predecessor, Mike Sargent. A site for a generator and data centre was identified in 2008. It aroused considerable public opposition and at the time of writing the project was at best in limbo. In the Legislative Assembly, the Labor Party opposed the joint venture. Mackay spent many hours seeking support from the three independents, Dave Rugendyke, Paul Osborne, and former Liberal Chief Minister Trevor Kaine.

Ultimately, Rugendyke voted for it, Osborne did not and Kaine, by then disaffected from the Liberals generally and Carnell in particular, voted for it.

Still, much administrative detail had to be clarified. The final agreement ran to hundreds of pages.

The documents establishing ActewAGL were duly signed by Carnell and Bleasel on 29 August 2000, what Mackay believes was a landmark day for Canberra.

The signing was preceded by public and union demonstrations opposing the sale of ACTEW and at least one acrimonious meeting in ACTEW's board room.

Commercial bank ABN Amro had been commissioned by the Carnell government to prepare a scoping study on the potential sale of ACTEW. Based on the study, which valued ACTEW at well over $1 billion, the government believed it could fund its superannuation liability and avoid the increasing risk from competition in the electricity market. Though its proposal did not include selling the ACT's water storages or sewage treatment plants, there was well founded concern that the ACT government would no longer receive the considerable annual dividends paid by ACTEW.

In an attempt to placate some concerns, a meeting including representatives of ABN Amro and trade unions was arranged. Mackay says the decision to bring the two warring parties into the same meeting room—black suits facing off against blue collars—was the dumbest thing he had ever seen.

The head of the ACT's Chief Minister's Department, Alan Thompson, was also there, as was Electrical Trades Union representative Neville Betts, who did not enjoy a reputation for diplomacy. The meeting descended to shouting and table thumping which culminated in Betts making highly derogatory and sexist remarks about Carnell. As Mackay recalls it, words such as "bitch" and "slut" were used. Thompson, who took offence at the Chief Minister's being spoken about in that way, leapt to his feet and invited Betts to meet him outside. As it happened, there was no meeting outside. "Neville never left his seat," says John Mackay. "Neville was a big bloke, much bigger than Alan. But Alan was pretty wiry and Neville probably assessed he might not come off too well."

The ACT Legislative Assembly voted against the sale of ACTEW. But thanks to its support later for the joint venture with AGL, ActewAGL was set up and the ACT Government continued to receive healthy dividends. ActewAGL also boasted a continued high level of customer service combined with electricity prices that were among the lowest in Australia.

Only a few years into his new job running ActewAGL, Mackay faced one of the greatest conundrums of his time as CEO. This began with an explanation by the head of the electricity network, Bob Gibbs, of a "pott head". In energy distribution the term had nothing to do with smoking cannabis and did not refer to Harry Potter tragics.

An electricity pott head is a cast iron apparatus about the size of a football, placed at the top of an electricity pole. They were primarily used where above ground wires were taken underground to cross roads—a common thing in Canberra, which had about 600 pott heads. And they were exploding. The force of these explosions was throwing fragments of cast iron up to 300 metres.

The news got worse. Cast iron from one of these explosions was found in a Belconnen pre-school. Another piece went through the front window of a house. Gibbs took Mackay for a drive to examine the aftermath of some of the pott head explosions.

"They were dreadful, ominous looking things. They looked like a bomb and they went off like a bomb." The explosions occurred after water leaked into the pott heads, mixed with tar and caused an electrical short with the 415 volt current. Although Gibbs estimated it would cost about $4 million to get rid of them, Mackay instructed Gibbs to have them replaced within the month. Gibbs said that would leave much of Canberra without electricity. There was a lasting solution to the problem, but the best he could manage was to replace about three a week.

In 1997 there had been public outrage over the death of Katie Bender, struck by a one kilogram fragment of steel thrown about 430 metres across Lake Burley Griffin during the demolition of the Royal Canberra Hospital. Mackay asked Gibbs if there were not a temporary engineering solution to protect the public during the replacement program. There was not.

Now, having been alerted to this new danger, John saw these potentially lethal devices all around Canberra—in shopping centres, people's front yards and in car parks. He faced a major dilemma: "I thought, if I tell the world about this, Canberra will come to a stop. Schools will have to close down, there will be people moving out of houses, it will be the most shocking mess throughout the city. So I decided not to tell anybody."

He asked Gibbs to identify the pott heads in the most potentially dangerous locations and to make their replacement a priority. There were about 200 on that priority list. John still agonises over his decision not to alert the public or even the government to the danger: "It is a risk I decided was worth taking but was not a risk I'd have ever been able to justify in retrospect." He acknowledges that anyone who knew about them would have been justified in notifying the media. But the city would have been a shambles for the following two years. Mackay, as a leader, made the decision for no personal benefit but for what he believed to be the greater good.

The consequences to him, and of course to anyone injured or killed by one of these bombs, would have been enormous. As it happened, all the pott heads were replaced, no one was injured and Canberra's daily life continued normally.

At other times, John's larrikin spirit got him into hot water at ACTEW. On one occasion he could not resist the bait when he heard an ABC radio report saying the ACT women's cricket team was trying to raise money to travel to a tournament in Tasmania and that the men's team had offered $2,000 if the women would clean the men's dressing rooms. Mackay phoned in and offered $4,000 but only if the women refused to do the cleaning for the men. This led to lots of favourable talk-back radio and lots of fun. But it wasn't so funny when highly critical calls started coming in from some powerful men including John Turner, who was a member of the cricket board and an ACTEW board member, and from ACT Chief Justice John Gallop. "Well before lunch time I was hiding in my office and not taking any calls."

With ACT Chief Minister Jon Stanhope, launching a green energy scheme.

At about the same time a sculptor created a very funny bronze of former Prime Minister John Howard dressed in a military uniform but with his slouch hat on back to front. John couldn't resist paying to have it temporarily installed outside the ACTEW shopfront where he posed with it. He also poked fun at Howard in a radio interview. It was only when Mackay took a call from ACTEW Chairman Jim Service that he realised there had been some unfortunate, unintended consequences, not least because Mackay and Service were to attend a special lunch hosted by Howard only a few days later to celebrate Service being made an Officer of the Order of Australia.

Mackay believes the success of the ActewAGL joint venture has exceeded everyone's expectations. Shortly before concluding his term as CEO and later as chairman, he said he was proud that, despite pricing regulation, ActewAGL would make an annual profit of about $150 million. This was about ten times what had been predicted when the joint venture was established about 13 years previously.

In its first 10 years, the joint venture paid more than $1 billion to the ACT government in dividends and other payments. It spread its tentacles into surrounding New South Wales regions, gaining some 15,000 gas and electricity customers in Nowra, Goulburn, Young and areas down to the Victorian border. This growth allowed for unprecedented levels of corporate sponsorship and support for charities, sporting groups and community organisations.

Mackay played a key role in purchasing the entire Nowra and Bombaderry gas network, despite considerable caution from his board. The business was purchased at low cost and at the time of writing was worth at least 20 times the purchase price. The merger helped to secure ActewAGL's largest individual gas customer, Shoalhaven Starches, which produces most of Australia's ethanol.

Coupled with this success, independent surveys showed that across Australia ActewAGL continued to deliver electricity at about the lowest cost, had the most reliable network and the happiest staff, and provided the best customer service.

"I am pretty proud of that." He remains also very proud of and grateful to the leadership team which played a key role in that success, including: Ivan Slavich, Noel Whitehill, Maria Storti, Carsten Larsen, Tania Hutchison, Asoka Wijeratne, Ian Macara, Gary Voss and Paul Walshe.

Under Mackay's leadership (although he says it was not his idea) ActewAGL introduced bundles of products. The more products people included in their bundle, the greater the discount. The connection with TransACT meant telecommunications and pay television products could be included with gas and electricity. This gave ActewAGL a considerable advantage over its electricity and gas competitors and was one of the major reasons for its retaining nearly all of the domestic energy market in Canberra.

Based on market research, ActewAGL offered a new type of green energy product, which was significantly more successful than an earlier version. Indeed, it quickly became one of Australia's most successful green energy products.

During his ten year reign as ActewAGL CEO, John considered resigning only once. Over the space of about a week the recently retired head of the Prime Minister's Department, Max Moore-Wilton, and his successor in the role, Peter Shergold, both rang, wanting him to take on the job of Secretary of the Department of Defence. He had major trepidations because they would want him to make significant reforms in the face of opposition from the military chiefs. He would have had to work much harder and earn less money. He accepted the challenge because it was a real honour to take on one of the biggest and most high profile jobs he could have imagined. But it all came to nothing. John assumes that Prime Minister Howard scotched his appointment because he did not want Defence shaken up in the way being proposed.

The potential appointment was reported in *The Canberra Times* and John has been ribbed about it by his mates ever since. They claim that he leaked the story.

13

IN THE REAL CANBERRA

John Mackay had not heard of TransACT when he began working at ACTEW. There had already been some publicity of an idea within ACTEW to establish a broadband network in Canberra, which had been overlooked by Telstra and Optus as they competed in larger state capitals with their rollouts of fibre optic cable.

Development of the TransACT business plan had begun in 1996 with a small team led by chief architect Robin Eckermann. Joe Ceccato, Robert Clarke and Jane Taylor worked with Eckermann under ACTEW executive Neville Smith.

The business model was to build an open access network many years before that approach attracted widespread interest around the world. Australia's National Broadband Network (NBN) later had a similar model.

By the time Mackay began as ACTEW CEO, plans were reasonably advanced for a trial of a fibre-optic network in the Canberra suburb of Aranda. Jim Service told Mackay that one of his priorities in the next 12 months should be to establish the trial and then to commercialise TransACT.

"I said, 'I will be able to do that, no trouble at all'." One of the first problems was that people such as Eckermann who had considerable knowledge of fibre-optic cable knew little of the practical tasks of rolling cable out. In some ways, the task in Canberra was easier because most power lines, particularly in older suburbs, ran along the back fences of properties.

Announcing the recruitment of Lauren Jackson, one of the best female basketballers in the world, to play for the Canberra Capitals.

That at least overcame the concern raised in some state capitals by people who objected to fibre-optic cable infrastructure spoiling their streetscapes. Nevertheless, building the network in Canberra would still require engineering work, including running cable under streets.

The task that Mackay had thought would be no trouble, proved otherwise, not least because those who managed the electricity network wanted to protect it. Mackay ended up refereeing numerous fights, with Eckermann and Smith on one side and the head of the electricity network Bob Gibbs on the other. "I remember one day just before a board meeting and my management team are tearing each other's throats out in the room next door. The board could actually hear them swearing and shouting at each other."

Fights between members of management teams were common in those first days at ACTEW. Late on a Friday afternoon, two managers not involved with TransACT came to to ask Mackay to settle the dispute between them. He said he would think about the matter over the weekend and that the solution would involve sacking one or both. They did not come to his office on the Monday pleading for a decision. "I ended up getting rid of both of them within the next six months."

The concept of hanging fibre-optic cable from existing power poles seemed simple enough, but those responsible for the electricity network were concerned that some poles would not withstand the extra weight and that the routine replacement of poles would be more complex.

The success of the Aranda trial supported plans to proceed throughout the city. Mackay, conscious of the financial risk, suggested to the board that financial partners would be required if the project were to proceed. A separate company, TransACT Capital Communications, was established and ACTEW was initially a 50 per cent shareholder.

Chief Minister Carnell gave her approval for ACTEW's putting $20 million into the project so readily that when Mackay went to see her about it she told him he would not need to sit down.

The two had previously sought interest in the project from Optus and Telstra, so it was necessary to seek venture capital. At about the same time, the joint venture between ACTEW and AGL was being finalised. AGL had just bought two broadband businesses, Dingo Blue and COMindico. AGL's leaders were delighted to have the opportunity to share in the establishment of TransACT and contributed $20 million, a decision they would later regret, as AGL did not profit from any of the three ventures.

Despite the financial risk that Mackay had identified, there was no difficulty raising sufficient capital to begin the commercial rollout of TransACT. Indeed, there were threats of legal action by those whose finance was not required.

Richard Vincent was appointed as the first head of TransACT, which was formally launched in 2001 at a lavish function at the Canberra Convention Centre. The project had barely begun when the dot-com bubble burst. Companies previously so eager to invest in TransACT would not even return phone calls, let alone provide the money they had committed.

There were many rumours, denied at the time, that TransACT was about to collapse. "It was a very, very rough time. We went within one day of going into receivership. I had written a speech to the staff. We were absolutely sunk."

In his car one night outside a Chinese restaurant, John Mackay negotiated a rescue package. While his wife and friends dined inside, he joined an international phone conference and was passed food through the car window. After about two hours, a refinancing arrangement was settled which saved TransACT for the time being, but did not provide adequate funding for the rollout of fibre-optic cable throughout Canberra to be completed.

Having persuaded AGL to put in another $25 million, Mackay was told by AGL's managing director that he would lose his ActewAGL job if the venture failed: "I lost some sleep in those couple of weeks."

He claims no credit for the vision of those such as Robin Eckermann, which gave rise to the establishment of TransACT, but he is sure that it would not have gone ahead without his involvement or without his saving it when it fell at the first hurdle. The board of ACTEW as well as Carnell and the ACT Government believed in the great benefits for Canberra. With TransACT, Canberra had broadband fibre-optic cable ten, possibly 20 years before it would otherwise have had that service. It made an important difference to many businesses and some householders.

As John puts it, "When TransACT was being established, Telstra and Optus were chasing each other down both sides of the streets in Melbourne and Sydney but could not give a stuff about Canberra. They were treating Canberra the same way they were treating Boggabri."

As a commercial proposition, TransACT was a failure. Even after it was saved, a great deal of time, stress and energy were required to make it profitable. This included having ActewAGL take over many of the functions to contain the cost of TransACT.

Even when TransACT turned a profit the gain was marginal. The business was close to being sold about six times when potential purchasers withdrew. Finally it was sold to Perth company iiNet for $60 million on 21 November 2011. By then, ACTEW alone had put $60 million into TransACT and the TransACT books were showing a small profit.

Before the dot-com bubble burst John was entitled to take a director's fee. Instead, he took share options in TransACT. "I remember saying to Colette, these share options, they are worth bugger all now but if I am not a millionaire within a year I will give the game away. This place is going to go gangbusters. And it did. Straight down the drain."

For all that, it was a tremendous experience: "I am not repentant at all about setting up TransACT. In fact I am very proud of it. But I lost a lot of sleep and a lot of hair."

People outside Canberra often say that Canberrans are out of touch with the rest of Australia. Yet Canberra also hosts a transient population, of politicians and many of their staff, whose time in the national capital is mostly spent cloistered inside Parliament House, dining in restaurants, then retreating to sleep in their apartments or hotel rooms.

Then there are the federal public servants who work in government departments and who make up about 50 per cent of Canberra's workforce. For many of them, particularly the more senior ones, their focus is largely on government policy as it affects the nation. It seems that many do not regard Canberra as home, even if they have lived in the city for years. Their knowledge of the city and their interest in its daily life tend to be limited.

John Mackay's experience was typical of this. Though he moved to Canberra in 1969 and participated in social activities with neighbours and workmates, it was not until he joined ACTEW that he found what he calls "the real Canberra".

"It struck me like a tonne of bricks in the first couple of months that I worked at ACTEW. I knew more about what was happening in Pitt Street or Collins Street than I did about what was happening in Canberra. I really wasn't connected with the town. I thought the world revolved around Federal Parliament house."

It was quickly evident that ACTEW's focus was totally on Canberra as a city, with almost no consideration about what was happening in Parliament. As a senior public servant, driving to work, John had always thought of the motorists with whom he shared the road as people like him on their way to a public service office or Parliament House.

Suddenly he became aware that they were just as likely to be on their way to a business meeting or to a workplace unconnected with the public service, and that much of daily life in Canberra had nothing to do with the federal bureaucracy or Parliament.

"The kind of people who rang me up wanting stuff—who we dealt with on a daily basis—were not the people I had ever had anything to do with before."

It might be a developer on the phone wanting water and electricity connected to a new hotel or housing development. And he was closely involved for the first time with Canberra's local government. "Kate Carnell I believe was a fabulous Chief Minister and is a friend to this day."

Carnell was the ACT's third Chief Minister. She served from 2 March 1995 to 18 October 2000. Brisbane-born, she gained a pharmacy degree from the University of Queensland in 1976 and moved to Canberra the following year. She bought a pharmacy in 1981 in Red Hill, and owned it until 2000.

From 1988 to 1994, she was the inaugural chair of the ACT branch of the Australian Pharmacy Guild and was national vice-president of the Guild from 1990 to 1994.

She joined the Liberal Party in 1991, was elected to the second ACT Legislative Assembly in 1992 and replaced Trevor Kaine as Leader of the Opposition in 1993.

Carnell and the government she led were severely and widely criticised over the death of Katie Bender, aged 12, when the decommissioned Royal Canberra Hospital was demolished by implosion on 13 July 1997 to make way for the National Museum of Australia.

An inquest found she had no personal responsibility for the death but the

With old friend John Preston, and Preston's magnificent steam tractor. The two men shared the driving at the head of several Canberra Day parades.

coroner found the government had turned the implosion into a public circus with the Chief Minister's approval.

Kate Carnell resigned as Chief Minister in October 2000, pre-empting a no confidence motion against her in the assembly over a massive cost overrun for the redevelopment of Bruce Stadium, now GIO Stadium. The project's $27.3 million budget included $12.3 million from the ACT Government and $15 million from the private sector. The redevelopment finally cost $82 million, funded entirely by the Government. The ACT Auditor-General found the original cost estimate had not undergone proper assessment, review or analysis.

Many years later, Carnell said that in resigning she had taken ministerial responsibility for breaches of the *Financial Management Act* related to the stadium redevelopment because it had occurred in her portfolio, although she had not known about the breaches.

Redevelopment of the stadium began in 1997 to prepare the venue for soccer matches as part of the 2000 Olympic Games based in Sydney. On 28 May 2000, snow fell during a rugby league match between the Canberra Raiders and Wests Tigers. The snow damaged the turf intended for the Olympic soccer.

To overcome the unsightly appearance of the playing surface, someone decided to paint it green. Whether or not Carnell was involved in this decision, she received much of the opprobrium that followed. John Mackay was a member of the Stadiums Authority at the time and reserves his harshest criticism for government bureaucrats who had no experience of running a stadium or of choosing the correct grass for the Canberra climate.

In the Australia Day Honours of 2006, Carnell was appointed an Officer of the Order of Australia (AO) for her services and contributions to the Australian Capital Territory.

John believes Kate was dealt some tough cards and in the end was treated harshly: "I was a paid-up member of her bandwagon and I applauded what she was doing."

As her support for TransACT demonstrates, she was prepared to take risks to develop the city. Facing crisis over the stadium redevelopment fiasco, she sought John's advice and after thinking the matter over, he wrote her a short note in which he suggested she should resign.

The roles were reversed many years later when she emailed him offering her support when he became embroiled in political controversy. In many ways it was his decision to resign as chair of ACTEW that led to the preparation of this book.

These days they have an occasional chuckle over the painting of the grass: "We have also chatted once or twice about the appointment of Rob Tonkin to replace John Walker as head of the Chief Minister's Department. She included me on the selection panel. I expressed doubts about Tonkin, but she went ahead and appointed him. On his first day in the job I invited him for a coffee and told him I had voted against him and told him why. I did this because I was sure he would find out, so he might as well get it straight from the horse's mouth. History will show that Tonkin was not great and was shuffled on after a few years."

Of Kate Carnell, John says there was never much doubt over what she was thinking. As head of ACTEW, he was frequently critical of decisions by the ACT's pricing regulator, the ACT Independent Competition and Regulatory Commission. Faced with a draft report on proposed electricity prices, Mackay phoned Carnell to say the Commissioner, then Paul Baxter, must be brought to heel. She responded that John must think she was an idiot and there was no way she would be doing any such thing.

14

HELPING A FIRE BLACKENED CITY

The first day of 2003 dawned hot and dry in Canberra. As the month unfolded, strong winds, high temperatures, low humidity and high fuel loads portended extreme fire danger and the city was on edge. At this time, the Mackay family was typical of many other Canberra families who forsook the city for the New South Wales south coast.

Fires began in the Brindabella and Namadgi National Parks west of Canberra on 8 January. Lightning strikes started 160 fires. On 13 January a helicopter that was water bombing fires in the forests west of the city crashed into Bendora Dam, injuring the pilot. ACT Chief Minister Jon Stanhope and Chief Fire Officer Peter Lucas-Smith were reviewing the fires from the Snowy Hydro Southcare helicopter. Its pilot positioned his craft over the dam so Stanhope, Lucas-Smith and a paramedic could dive in and rescue the injured pilot. The three and the helicopter pilot received awards for their bravery.

Their bravery and endurance greatly boosted the morale of Canberra residents, for whom the oppressive heat and fire danger had become a daily struggle.

Informally, by Wednesday 15 January, emergency service staff were expressing to this writer grave concerns over the risk to the city. This was in sharp contrast to remarks seven days previously that there would be divine intervention to put out the fires, as in the previous year, with a summer storm.

On 17 January, still with no major public warning about the imminent danger, Canberra's main bushfire logistical support was moved from Bulls Head and the Ororral Valley, well beyond Canberra's outskirts, to the North Curtin District Playing Fields, only a few kilometres from the centre of the city, a sign of the looming danger.

The next day, 18 January, was hot and windy. The temperature climbed to 40 degrees and wind speeds to more than 60 km/h.

Two fires in the Namadgi National Park were out of control. The park and the Tidbinbilla Nature Reserve were closed. Burned leaves were falling on southern Canberra suburbs by about 9 a.m. and at about 2 p.m. police evacuated Tharwa, a small village south of Canberra.

Firefighters under the command of ACT Rural Fire Service Southern Brigades Captain Val Jeffrey prevented the loss of any property in Tharwa except for some minor sheds. Jeffrey, with many years' experience of bushfires, was later a sharp critic of the lack of preparation for a major fire.

Stanhope declared a state of emergency at 2.45 pm on 18 January and within a few hours more than 500 houses and four lives had been lost. Fire and extreme winds brought down powerlines, leaving large parts of the city without electricity. Water, gas and telephones were unavailable to several suburbs and the city's main sewage treatment plant was temporarily shut down, risking the discharge of untreated sewage into the Murrumbidgee River.

Bushfires that swept into Canberra in January 2003 devastated the power supply network.

Prime Minister John Howard and John Mackay thank emergency workers as Canberra recovers from the fires.

Far more detailed histories of this event and its aftermath are recorded elsewhere. This summary is included here to illustrate the challenge that John Mackay faced on his interrupted south coast holiday: "The week or so before the fires I was getting emails at our holiday home at Broulee. They were getting more and more serious. I lay awake on the Friday night with trepidation about the following day."

On the Saturday morning of the firestorm, as he walked on the beach with Colette, he told her of his fears and she readily agreed to return to Canberra with him.

By early afternoon, he was with his management team in ActewAGL's emergency control room in Fyshwick.

"Horror unfolded over the next few hours and we became acquainted with what had happened through that afternoon and into the night. I stayed in the control room until after dawn on Sunday when it progressively emerged that we had a thousand poles on the ground; thousands of gas and electricity customers off supply; no operational sewerage system and even some people with no water."

"Over the next ten days, with lots of help, we restored all of this infrastructure. I spent lots of time dealing with my management team, our workers and the community through radio, television and *The Canberra Times* every day."

While all that was going on, there were also Actew AGL staff in need of support after losing their houses, and a personal loss: "My heart broke when my wife phoned to say my little dog had died."

John had just enough time to get back to work, at ActewAGL's Tuggeranong depot where Prime Minister John Howard and ACT Chief Minister Jon Stanhope had come to thank the troops.

ActewAGL made a foundation gift of $250,000 to the bushfire appeal and helped to raise another $350,000 from a telethon run from its call centre.

John joined the appeal board and helped to raise $9 million and to develop criteria for distributing the money. He later joined the board chaired by Sandy Hollway that advised the government on what to do with the burned-out rural settlements of Uriarra, Stromlo and Tidbinbilla. The board also advised the government to establish an arboretum.

Soon after joining ACTEW, Mackay substantially increased its sponsorship of community organisations. The guidelines when he started dictated that ACTEW sponsorship was effectively limited to organisations with some connection to engineering.

With Gough Whitlam in front of Jackson Pollock's famous painting Blue Poles, which the National Gallery of Australia was able to purchase thanks to Whitlam's support.

With friend and powerbroker, Max Moore-Wilton, at the National Gallery of Australia, at the launch of the Turner to Monet exhibition in 2008.

Sharing a joke at a fund raiser with Prime Minister John Howard.

"I immediately turned that on its head. I could see tremendous opportunities for ACTEW to take on a much broader role." Chief Minister Carnell and ACTEW Chairman Jim Service strongly encouraged this change in direction. The motivation to increase sponsorship was twofold—to be a good corporate citizen, but perhaps more importantly to strengthen the commercial position of ACTEW and later of ActewAGL.

One of the early sponsorships which Mackay approved was the exhibition by US glass sculptor Dale Chihuly at the Australian National Gallery. After the Director of the Gallery, Brian Kennedy, persuaded him to sponsor the exhibition, "Chihuly: Masterworks in Glass", Mackay realised that the sponsorship was good for ACTEW as well as the Gallery and the exhibition. The exhibition, coinciding with Floriade, Canberra's spring festival of flowers, was extremely successful. It drew many visitors to Canberra and benefitted businesses including hotels, restaurants and taxis.

Mackay was quick to point out to these beneficiaries that it would be in their best interests to continue to buy their electricity from ACTEW, whose sponsorship contributed to their commercial gain. Sponsorship of exhibitions such as this also gave him the opportunity to entertain ACTEW customers at the gallery.

ActewAGL kept a far higher percentage of its commercial customers than most of its interstate competitors and it retained about 98 per cent of domestic customers. Electricity retailers, particularly in the state capitals, had lost more than 50 per cent of their customers and were also subject to considerable customer turnover. Mackay believed sponsorship contributed to customer retention.

Ultimately, the Gallery sponsorship was designed to promote ActewAGL as part of the Canberra and capital region community. It was also intended to ensure that Canberrans and visitors had the benefit of events and exhibitions that otherwise might not have come to the city.

Sponsorship later extended to major and minor sporting teams. Although sponsorship was good for business, there were times when Mackay agreed to offer support out of sympathy.

One of his principles as a manager was to treat staff something like his family. He had, from time to time, given financial support to individual staff members faced with a family crisis. This aroused some criticism from people who believed he was over-generous with public money.

Mackay acknowledges that he had made errors of judgement but remains steadfastly unrepentant of his decisions to arrange financial support to people in need, even when the contributions had come effectively from public money. "I felt always that without damaging ActewAGL at all, I could do a huge amount in the community just because we are such a big, powerful corporate body."

Using the resources of ActewAGL, he arranged an upgrade of information technology for the disability support organisation Koomarri. "Fixing Koomarri was just a drop in the ocean for us but for them was a tremendously big improvement to the way they could run their operation."

He insisted that such generosity did not contribute to an increase in electricity prices. But to those who felt it did, he said: "If they feel it put up their electricity bill they should nip out to Queanbeyan where they can get their electricity for twelve hundred bucks a year more. And instead of getting the best customer service and the most reliable supply they can have the 19th best customer service and the 26th most reliable supply. It is easy to criticise something in isolation but I see this stuff as a complete package."

Mackay said it was possible to meet all of these goals: to run an organisation with the best management practice, to create a happy and cohesive workforce, to provide high quality customer service, to look after staff as though they were family, and to offer sponsorships and contributions to the community.

His approach could be fairly contrasted with the frequent criticism of corporate greed, and of running companies to maximise profits while contributing little if anything to the communities in which they operate. Mackay argues that there is a twofold gain when corporations, government or private, help individuals and organisations through sponsorship or direct support. Giver and receiver both benefit.

It was the same with the hot air balloon he arranged for wheelchair passengers. Although it was not within the remit of the Australian Protective Service, the involvement greatly boosted the morale of staff as well as benefitting Camp Quality. "It was great for Camp Quality, it was great for the APS image and it was a fantastic rallying point for our staff. Why wouldn't you do that? I am critical of someone who would go into that role and not think outside the walls of traditional management. I don't think they would get as good a result as I would with that broader view."

Canberra's pricing regulator, the ACT Independent Competition and Regulatory Commission, has criticised Canberra's water utility, Actew Water, for providing sponsorship. The Commission's view was that Actew Water had no competition and therefore gained nothing by sponsorship.

Mackay counters that without this sponsorship, Canberra would have no symphony orchestra. Certainly, the money could come from government, but with the competing demands for government funds, such largesse is uncertain. And perhaps the most important benefit of this sponsorship was

John Mackay's final night as CEO of ActewAGL at a gathering in 2008 of 1,500 staff, with his long serving executive assistant, Carol Peake. The theme of the night was "dress in black".

to the self image of Actew Water's staff: "They feel like they are working for someone who cares about the broader picture of Canberra and not just the molecules coming out of the tap."

Naturally, good work requires good support. Throughout his time as head of ACTEW and ActewAGL, Mackay was served by his secretary, the larger than life Carol Peake, who first served John when he was Deputy Secretary at the Department of Administrative Services.

"What she did for me must never be underestimated. She sent a picture of me out to the world which was incredibly positive." She also proved to be most efficient, and generally protected her boss from callers he did not wish to see or speak to. Once a disgruntled staff member who was always complaining about other managers got through Carol's screen. She announced the caller and John said something like, "Don't put that fucking idiot through to me." She already had. "So the first part of my conversation was assuring him that I was not talking about him."

One day a visitor to his office complained that Mackay continually referred to him as a liar. Mackay assured his visitor that not only was he not being called a liar, but that he was not a liar.

The visitor responded, "You told a friend of mine you would not trust me to take your dog for a walk around the block."

Mackay agreed he probably had said that, and added a helpful clarification: "That is because I think you are incompetent—I wouldn't get the dog back."

Eventually, after about ten years as CEO of ACTEW and ActewAGL, during which time he built around him, he said, "the best management team you could ever imagine", Mackay felt the time for a change was near.

At the beginning of each year, he spent several weeks at the coast relaxing and reflecting. On his return to Canberra he would assail his staff with his plans and aspirations for the coming year. After about ten years, he noticed several of his team looking out the window during his pep talk, clearly believing they had heard all this before. There were other indicators, including the safety record which, after years of continual improvement, showed a slight decline.

"I could have stayed on as CEO for another five years, no trouble at all. But I just thought, I should get out at my peak rather than hang on and have people asking, 'When is he going to leave?'."

Around the same time Jim Service told Mackay of his plans to resign as chairman of ActewAGL, ACTEW and TransACT on 30 June 2008. So Mackay suggested he would resign as CEO and that he wished to be appointed chair of the three organisations. Service said there were many reasons why this change would not normally be considered, but in this case he believed it would work. Chief Minister Stanhope agreed and the change was made.

Michael Costello, the previous head of ACTEW Corporation, replaced Mackay as CEO of ActewAGL. The former Secretary of the Department of Veterans Affairs, Mark Sullivan, in turn replaced Costello as head of ACTEW Corporation. In his new role, Mackay stood back for some months to ensure he fulfilled the chairman's role, not the CEO's role.

In September 2007, while John was still CEO, he and Colette drove from Canberra to visit Betty in Dubbo Hospital. They found her in a dreadful state, due to a lack of proper care while in hospital. John, through his great friend Dr Peter Yorke, arranged for her to be flown to Canberra that afternoon, with one of Australia's leading specialists ready to operate. But Betty refused: "Don't do that. I'll be DOA if you do."

John and his siblings Anne, Phil and Liz were with Betty in the early hours a few days later when she died. Her funeral was conducted by her good friend Ross Godfrey—the Presbyterian minister in Wellington who had also given Jack's eulogy in 1980. John's eulogy for Betty he describes as one of the best speeches he has ever made, and one that would have made her proud. He and Betty were very close, sharing a similar sense of humour and serendipitous approach to life.

15

WATER FOR A THIRSTY CITY

Shortly before these changes, on 20 May 2008, Jon Stanhope launched the Bulk Water Alliance, formed between ACTEW, GHD, Abigroup and John Holland. The task of the alliance was to design and construct a new dam on the Cotter River, a Murrumbidgee to Googong Reservoir pipeline and an upgrade of the Googong Dam spillway. The three projects were estimated then to cost about $300 million.

Exactly who estimated the cost of those three projects is not known but it certainly was not ACTEW's new managing director, Mark Sullivan, whose appointment was announced on June 3 that year and who did not assume his new position until July 1. And it was not John Mackay, who did not assume chairmanship of ACTEW until the same day. But the ultimate cost of those projects would see Sullivan initially and Mackay later subject to public and political criticism.

In mid-2008, the $300 million was little more than an estimate and had certainly not been subject to the rigour of a competitive tender. Nor did it take account of delays associated with obtaining numerous approvals for the Cotter dam and the pipeline, which contributed greatly to their cost increase.

Water restrictions began in Canberra in 2002 and became successively harsher. In a major presentation on 30 April 2004, ACTEW managing director Michael Costello announced the beginning of consultation between ACTEW and the community about whether the ACT needed a new water supply; if so, when; and from where.

Flood waters played havoc with construction of the new Cotter Dam in 2012.

He told his audience, "Now you may say that given the low risks involved, why make extensive plans for contingency? Let me tell you something. Whether it is short term or long term, I do not plan to be the managing director of ACTEW who, in some years' time, informs the people of Canberra that they are about to run out of water, or that they are in their third successive year of Stage 5 restrictions, but please excuse us because there was not a high risk that this would ever happen."

In late December 2004 ACTEW issued a report to the ACT Government recommending a new water source for the ACT. The report did not indicate ACTEW's preferred option but made clear that projected population growth and climate change dictated that existing water storages could not meet future needs.

However, on 12 August 2005, Costello said based on conservative projections, the ACT would have enough water until at least 2023 without a new dam. Speaking at a Canberra Business Council lunch, he said even if it were found that more water was needed, there would be plenty of time to build more storage. But he was confident transferring water to Googong Dam from the Cotter catchment and possibly from the Murrumbidgee River would prove more successful than previously estimated.

Not only was there not plenty of time, but by May 2007 water storages had fallen almost to 30 per cent of capacity and there was genuine fear, not least on Costello's part, that Canberra would run out of water. On 15 May 2007 he had the melancholy job of announcing all outdoor use of potable water would be banned from 1 July or sooner in Canberra and Queanbeyan with even more drastic measures being considered, including restrictions within the home. "We are heading for what is easily going to be our worst year of inflows on record."

The situation was so serious that not even limited outdoor watering would be permitted. Above average rain in June came just in time to avoid these austerities but strict water restrictions continued for about another three and a half years.

This was the background to the Government's eventual approval of the construction of the enlarged dam on the Cotter and the pipeline to transfer water from the Murrumbidgee to Googong reservoir.

Construction of the pipeline began in January 2011, by which time the projected cost had increased by about $4.6 million, a three per cent increase blamed on delays in having the project approved.

When the pipeline was commissioned on 24 August 2012, water storages were at about 99 per cent of capacity and for at least the next two years there was to be no practical need to transfer water to Googong reservoir. Indeed the reservoir overflowed early in 2014. There was little if any public or political acknowledgement that the project was completed about 15 per cent under budget.

By contrast, there was a major row over the cost of the Cotter dam which increased from the eventual estimate of $363 million to about $410 million. In a bitter irony, heavy rain, for which Canberra had prayed for eight years, fell in December 2010, inundating the construction site and delaying work. Then in March 2012, with the dam wall only half its final 80 m height, another flood caused major damage to the construction and machinery. All the scaffolding was effectively destroyed and with the site unsafe, work ceased for about three months.

In 2009, before work on the dam began, Mark Sullivan had predicted that the best way to break a drought was to build a dam. By March 2011 he acknowledged that his prayers for rain had gone too far.

The increased costs by all the rain were exacerbated by a geological fault identified in about May 2011, the extent of which could not have been foreseen when the project began. To create a stable foundation for the dam, 12,000 cubic metres of rock was removed and the subsequent 9 m deep hole filled with 12,000 cubic metres of concrete. This work and the delay of about three months to construction added about $10 million to the cost of the project.

The mounting cost put public pressure on Mackay and Sullivan. Sullivan said, "The Cotter Dam was my introduction to controversy in Canberra. I took the dam as I got it and tried to make sense of it." The Cotter Dam issue might seem minor now to people who know about the next big controversy that would break over the two men.

After the second flood and subsequent political wrangling over the increasing cost, chief executive of the Australian Water Association Tom Mollenkopf said Sullivan had handled the crisis well. "Mark has been a great ambassador for calm heads."

It is hard to escape the belief that Sullivan and Mackay were made scapegoats over the cost increase, some of which would have been avoided had the Government approved the project several years sooner.

By July 2004, inflows to ACT water storages for the previous five years were at an all time low, marking Canberra's worst drought on record. Yet the drought was to continue for another five years.

The ACT Liberal Party went to the 2004 election with a commitment to build a dam on the Naas River, south of Canberra. That commitment was based on work done in 1968 by the Commonwealth Department of Works. It is not possible to know now what the Liberals would have done had they won the election but their preferred site for a new dam was later shown to be quite inferior to enlarging the Cotter dam.

It was not until 2007 that the government supported construction of a new dam. Without that delay, flooding of the worksite would not have occurred and when the rain came the new reservoir would have filled. Nevertheless, from the decision in 2007 to completion of the Cotter dam, it is the fastest dam of its size to be built in Australia and when the next drought comes, Sullivan and Mackay will be able to look with justifiable pride at the result of their commitment to the project.

16

PLANTING THE SEEDS FOR A VISIONARY PROJECT

After Canberra's 2003 firestorm, John Mackay was asked to join the public appeal committee chaired by then Anglican Bishop of Canberra and Goulburn George Browning, to help distribute about $9 million raised by the public appeal.

At about the same time, the ACT Government established the Bushfire Recovery Taskforce, chaired by Sandy Hollway. It later established the Non-Urban Study Steering Committee, also chaired by Hollway. That committee reported in August 2003 and, among other things, proposed an arboretum on Dairy Farmers Hill.

The 250 hectare site previously included a semi-commercial pine plantation run by the ACT Government. It was largely destroyed by a bushfire in December 2001, which probably prevented the complete destruction of the site less than 13 months later by the 2003 firestorm.

In January 2004 the ACT Government established a committee, also chaired by Hollway, known as Shaping Our Territory, to advise in more detail on implementation of plans for the burned out rural villages and nature parks. Dairy Farmers Hill was included on the agenda for that Committee, which advised the Government until June 2005.

Mackay was a committee member and became a passionate supporter of the proposed arboretum. During the committee's preparation of its *Shaping Our Territory* report, opinion varied on whether an arboretum should be exclusively of native Australian trees or largely of an international flavour. Mackay favoured the latter and ultimately that is what was proposed to the Government. During a lively debate, Mackay said: "We already have an Australian native arboretum. It's called the Pilliga Scrub."

Having visited the Butchart Gardens on Vancouver Island in Canada, Mackay shared the enthusiasm of prominent Canberra businessman Eric Koundouris for establishing an arboretum on what had become effectively a wasteland. After all, the Butchart Gardens were established in a quarry after its limestone deposits were exhausted.

Robert Pim Butchart, a pioneer in the North American cement industry, developed the quarry and built a cement plant in 1904. About two years later, as the limestone ran out, his wife Jennie arranged for soil to be brought to fill the pit and began to establish the now world famous gardens.

It wasn't John Mackay who thought of an international arboretum in Canberra but he soon embraced the idea, and together with Eric Koundouris he pursued Stanhope to gain support for the project.

The idea appealed to Stanhope, but Canberra was still recovering from the firestorm and was experiencing a major drought. No one could know it then, but the drought would continue until late 2010.

In September 2004, the committee published a report, *Canberra International Arboretum and Gardens—Design Ideas Competition*. About 45 entries were displayed in Canberra's Albert Hall in February 2005. On 31 May that year, Stanhope announced Taylor Cullity Lethlean Landscape Architects, in conjunction with Tonkin Zulaikha Greer Architects, were winners, with their "100 Forests, 100 Gardens" concept design.

A permanent board for the Canberra International Arboretum and Gardens was established in August of that year. Chaired by Sandy Hollway, the board's role was to oversee the implementation of the winning design. The board, of which Mackay was a member, took advice from tree specialists and in turn advised the Government on the type of trees to plant. The board oversaw the planting of the first ten forests.

The development of the arboretum received a major blow in 2007. Facing an election the following year, the ACT Government was under considerable pressure. First, the drought, which the previous year had taken Canberra within a few weeks of having all outdoor use of water banned, had caused the closure of many public sports areas. The watering ban was averted but already many private gardens and lawns had died for lack of water. There was at least the perception that scarce water should not be used on the arboretum while the public faced major water restrictions.

Secondly, seeking to save money, the Government had announced the

Richard Moffatt's steel sculpture of an eagle's nest, chosen by John for the National Arboretum Canberra in 2008. The popular sculpture sits atop Dairy Farmers Hill. (Picture by William Hall)

closure of about 40 schools in Canberra.

In October 2007, ACT Opposition Leader Bill Stefaniak said that the Government had engaged in numerous wasteful projects. Among these he included the arboretum.

Stanhope and the Government faced widespread criticism for allocating water and money to the arboretum while residents lived with water restrictions and many were losing their neighbourhood schools. Stanhope disbanded the arboretum board and the project went into abeyance.

But some people were still keen on the arboretum. John Mackay salvaged a demountable building and had it installed on the arboretum site. Some trees were planted and a steel contemporary sculpture in the form of an eagle's nest, with eagle, found a home there.

Though the drought continued, Stanhope retained his enthusiasm for the arboretum and, with anger over the school closures at least subsiding, asked Mackay to promote interest in the arboretum amongst the diplomatic community.

Stanhope hosted a major diplomatic and business function on 15 April 2008 at the arboretum site, to seek financial support. Mackay was there, ostensibly to speak about water, or the lack of it. During a break in proceedings, Stanhope asked him to chair a board of governors with Eric Koundouris, Professor of Forestry Peter Kanowski, and farmer and land advocate Sherry McArdle-English as core members, not least to draw some of the political flak away from Stanhope's office.

Former senior ACT public servant Jocelyn Plovits later became secretary to the board. Former ACT tourism executive David Marshall, later a media and communications strategist, and the head of the Village Building Company and major donor to the Liberal Party, Bob Winnel, also joined the board and contributed about $2.5 million. Former CEO of the National Botanic Gardens, Anne Duncan, joined some time later.

Despite public criticism and continuing drought, the ACT bureaucracy was enthusiastic about the arboretum, which had begun humbly enough. Money was found here and there and some unused display sheds were obtained from the ACT Land Development Agency. About 100,000 cubic metres of soil surplus to requirements for construction of the Gungahlin Drive Extension was offered for use at the arboretum and welcomed with the condition it be dumped in the shape of an amphitheatre.

So in the early days, the formation of the arboretum more or less followed the principle of begging, borrowing and stealing. However, the ACT allocated significant funding after the 2008 re-election of the Stanhope government. Then, a major step forward came with a $20 million grant from the Federal Government, part of a birthday gift for Canberra's centenary in 2013. The grant was announced by Prime Minister Julia Gillard when she planted a tree at the arboretum on 19 April 2011.

Accompanied by Stanhope, she planted a ghost gum (*Corymbia aparrerinja*) in the central valley of the arboretum. This species, which had symbolic and actual roots traced to the foundation of the Australian Labor Party, was no ordinary tree. It was a sapling grown from a cutting from "The Tree of Knowledge", which once grew next to the railway station in the central western Queensland town of Barcaldine. There striking shearers met in 1891 to protest against their poor working conditions and wages. The shearers' strike led to the formation of the Australian Workers Union and ultimately the Australian Labor Party.

As support began to grow, Jocelyn Plovits and others founded the Friends of the Arboretum, which quickly boasted more than 1,500 members. Colette Mackay was soon devoting about three days a week as secretary of the Friends.

Visits by celebrities, most of whom planted trees, raised the profile of the arboretum, as did the establishment of a research project there by the ANU.

The National Arboretum Canberra was formally opened on 1 February 2013. The arboretum is west of Scrivener Dam on the Molonglo River, which

Ban Ki Moon, Secretary-General of the United Nations, with John at the National Arboretum Canberra, preparing to plant the symbol of peace, an olive tree. At left is Chief Minister, Katy Gallagher.

forms Lake Burley Griffin. The site is only a few kilometres from Civic and a similar distance from Parliament House. Visitors can inspect nearly 100 forests of species from around the world that are rare or emblematic and endangered. Visitors enjoy 360 degree views which take in the city and the Brindabella ranges.

It quickly developed into one of Canberra's major attractions, with about 500,000 visitors in its first 12 months—about 30 per cent more than visited the long established National Botanic Gardens during the same period.

Although they had made do with temporary structures, the board pressed for permanent buildings to be built to the highest standard or not at all. "Think wow," John Mackay told the architects for the visitors' centre, and David Marshall said, "Think big."

At the heart of the arboretum is the village centre, which includes a gift shop, café and restaurant. Although the building cost about $14 million, John says that it was a bargain: "I think it is a building which will stand the test of time."

It has a domed roof of more than 2,000 square metres and floor to ceiling windows along 60 metres at the front, giving excellent views of Lake Burley

Griffin, Parliament House, Telstra Tower and Woden. It can accommodate functions with 500 people seated or 900 standing.

The architects also designed a stunning pavilion for reflection, a non-denominational chapel later named "The Margaret Whitlam Pavilion". Mackay was disappointed that the design of the pavilion was considerably scaled back before construction.

He was proud of the children's play area beside the visitors' centre. He said it was among the best play areas in the world. It had the personal backing of ACT Chief Minister Katy Gallagher, who, with young children, quickly realised that families would not visit if there were no entertainment for children.

Fortunately, more than 60 per cent of the Himalayan cedar forest on the site remained after the 2001 bushfire and the 2003 firestorm. So too did the cork oak plantation whose history dates almost to the establishment of Canberra.

The history of those plantings is recorded by Susan Parsons in "Tree Stories" on the arboretum website: www.nationalarboretum.act.gov.au/visit/trees/tree stories.

Walter Burley Griffin recognised the potential of cork oak for Canberra's dry climate and, in 1916, sent a supply of acorns to Yarralumla Nursery for a trial by Charles Weston. These were sourced from the Royal Botanic Gardens Melbourne and planted in October 1917 at the "Green Hills Area Cork Oak Reserve".

A larger shipment of acorns was sent from Spain, but the ship carrying them, the SS *Boorara*, was torpedoed and sank. A replacement shipment arrived soon after and, by 1920, 9600 cork oaks were planted at Green Hills on an 8 hectare site. They have been thinned several times and about 3000 healthy trees remain.

Early landscaping at the arboretum included a dam which, despite the drought, quickly filled with water. Part of the explanation for that is that water from another dam had to be disposed of, and John as head of ActewAGL was asked how that could be done without discharging it into the Murrumbidgee River. He quickly recognised the opportunity of directing it to the arboretum. That water in the dam helped to allay public concern over the use of water at the arboretum at a time when most private Canberra gardens were ravaged by drought.

At time of writing, most of the trees at the arboretum are barely a few metres tall. Of course, predicting the future is an inexact science. But John Mackay was satisfied. "I imagine in 50 years it will be as important to Canberra as Central Park is to New York or as Hyde Park is to Sydney or as

Hyde Park is to London. It will increasingly be more in the centre of Canberra. It will be a place where people go for dozens of reasons—some of which will be an interest in nature and some of which will be just a damn nice place to go to have a cup of coffee. It will be a jewel in the crown of Australia, I have no doubt at all about that."

He likes the audacious plan to plant 100 gardens at the arboretum, but says the suggested move of the annual Floriade festival there would be an embuggerance. "I think at some time in the future we will make Floriade completely redundant because we will have Floriade all year round. That might not come for 50 years but it will come."

Enthusiastic and lateral thinking people, including public servants, business people and Chief Minister Jon Stanhope did much to get the arboretum established. Without Stanhope, the project would not even have begun. Much of the early thinking and planning occurred as he walked around the site with Mackay, who says "No Jon, no arboretum." Their informal discussions helped to avoid bureaucratic obstruction.

Mackay believes that Stanhope and his successor, Katy Gallagher, who was then treasurer, were the only two members of the government who were genuinely enthusiastic about the project. Stanhope had to persuade his cabinet to stump up more than $40 million—a difficult task given the other demands on the ACT budget.

"Jon and I were very, very close. We spoke frequently; we walked frequently; he or his office would ring and ask for me to do something or not to do something as the case may be. I felt I owed him that; he was the guy elected to run the territory so why wouldn't I be jumping around to help him to do what he was elected to do?"

"In those days, Stanhope was besotted with two things—the arboretum and the glassworks—and he put me in charge of both of them. This was a tremendous thing for him to do and he obviously thought I had a reasonably safe pair of hands and that I would push them with every breath in me."

Mackay also supported Stanhope's enthusiasm for public art. He took Stanhope to dinner in Sydney one night and showed him "The Vase of Plenty" sculpture. Mackay worked with Latin American ambassadors to help to establish the Latin American Plaza in Canberra. He commissioned a sculpture for the foyer of the new ActewAGL building and played a major role in developing the new glass chimney at Canberra Glassworks as well as several sculptures at the arboretum.

At Jon Stanhope's farewell as Chief Minister, the master of ceremonies was John Mackay. Stanhope named Mackay then as one of three people to whom he owed most during his term. So, from what had been a shaky beginning

Senator Margaret Reid, businessman Terry Snow and John were inducted into the Canberra Honour Walk in 2010.

in their relationship, this was "not too bad". The shaky beginning Mackay attributes to having been an unashamed fan of Stanhope's Liberal predecessor, Kate Carnell. "I think there were some doubts about my political allegiance. Although anybody who knows me knows I have voted Labor all my life and have quite a strong left wing bent on most things."

Ultimately, Mackay was one of Stanhope's confidantes when Stanhope was deciding whether to step down as Chief Minister. At the time, the University of Canberra was going to appoint Mackay as Chancellor. Stanhope declined when Mackay suggested he could take that position instead.

Later Stanhope's successor, Katy Gallagher, appointed Stanhope to the board of the arboretum. This, it seems, was the catalyst for the souring of the relationship between the two men. Mackay offered to step down as chairman of the board in favour of Stanhope but he declined the offer.

Stanhope behaved quite badly on the arboretum board in Mackay's view: "He would make some very strong points, shout down people who did not agree with him, then leave. He came to only four or five meetings but none of them were happy meetings. All of our previous meetings, though we had some differences, were very happy and enthusiastic. We had four or five meetings that Jon attended where the mood was appalling."

By this time the two of them had embraced different approaches to developing the arboretum. Stanhope's major focus was on the trees while Mackay's was on the infrastructure and on making the arboretum a highly successful attraction for visitors. Mackay considered resigning and their friendship shared over almost ten years was disintegrating.

Nevertheless, Mackay, as Chancellor of the University of Canberra, enthusiastically supported the appointment of Stanhope as an adjunct professor at the university.

In 2011, Stanhope was appointed administrator of Christmas Island and the two men have rarely spoken since. One of those occasions was at the formal opening of the arboretum. They shook hands and in his speech, Mackay acknowledged Stanhope as the father of the arboretum.

After Stanhope left for Christmas Island, Mackay sent him an email acknowledging their once fantastic relationship was not in good shape: "I regard that as entirely my fault and I hope at some stage in the future we can get together and get on with our friendship." He still harbours the hope.

Stanhope had made Mackay Canberra Citizen of the Year in 2009 and included him in the Canberra Honour Walk in 2010, and Mackay feels grateful. "I regret the fact we have gone from friendship to nothing and that occurred within about six months after he ceased to be Chief Minister."

Stanhope declined to go on the record in this book about their relationship.

Mackay advised Katy Gallagher he would not seek reappointment to the arboretum board when his term expired in August 2014.

17

CULTURE, HEALTH AND EDUCATION

C anberra Glassworks is one of the few Australian cultural centres wholly dedicated to contemporary glass art. It was officially opened by Jon Stanhope on 25 May 2007, with the highly dedicated Ann Jakle as its founding CEO.

In Wentworth Avenue, Kingston, the glassworks is on the site of Canberra's first power station, built between 1913 and 1915. It generated electricity until 1957 and is Canberra's oldest public building.

The glassworks was one of Stanhope's pet projects and another for which he sought assistance from John Mackay who chaired the board of the glassworks for about five years and remains proud of the role he and ActewAGL played in helping to establish this successful venture.

The world-class community of active glass artists in Canberra was greatly stimulated by the School of Art Glass Workshop at the Australian National University. Glassmakers were looking for a permanent home and finally persuaded the ACT Government that the old power station would be a suitable venue. The link between the former power station and ActewAGL was obvious.

Many years ago, the 20 m chimney at the power station was demolished. The new use of the building is recognised in a significant piece of public art in its place, a 20 m glass chimney. ActewAGL was a major sponsor of this work. The glassworks has a public viewing gallery above the main hot-shop areas, and public walkways around all of the glassworking areas. Visitors can meet

The hot shop at Canberra Glassworks in 2011.

artists, see glassmaking, view exhibitions and even work with glass.

Opportunities to make other contributions to Canberra kept arising. As ActewAGL CEO, Mackay was approached by his chairman, Jim Service, to chair a committee which aimed to raise $1 million for the city's Calvary Hospital. Typically, John decided to give the daunting task a go. "So I rounded up some mates." One was Jim Murphy, a prominent Canberra citizen who died in 2011, aged 63. Best known for his liquor outlets, Jim Murphy's Market Cellars, he was also widely respected for his charitable work.

Mackay kicked off the appeal, having encouraged ActewAGL to make a donation. Murphy and Mackay knocked on many doors, spoke to many people and held many meetings. "We ended up raising effectively $1 million, which was an eye-opener to me."

No doubt as a result of this success, Mackay was invited to chair Calvary's community council, on which he served for several years.

Responding to an invitation from a sister of the Little Company of Mary, Mackay went to Sydney, where he was invited to become a director of the national board of the Little Company of Mary Health Care. He accepted and at his first board meeting developed suspicions over the financial state of the operation. These were confirmed at the next meeting, when it became clear the business was heading for a significant loss. "In my opinion it had gone from a small family business through a series of acquisitions to a serious national company. But it was still being managed as though it was a small family business."

Some of those acquisitions, including the John James Hospital in Canberra, now Calvary John James, were unsustainable. The organisation had paid high prices and it was apparent to the board that drastic action was required to avert serious financial trouble.

So successful was the board's action that the crisis ended and the Little Company of Mary Health Care established a solid financial foundation with a $1 billion annual turnover.

As the only non-Catholic on the board John had no difficulty understanding, living and embracing Catholic principles: "I even had a part in us developing our own prayer for the board."

His experience in buying and selling property offered a pragmatic approach to the buying and selling of property by the Little Company of Mary Health Care.

Calvary Hospital in Canberra, opened in 1979, is operated by Calvary Health Care ACT, a not for profit venture of the Little Company of Mary Health Care on behalf of the ACT Government.

However, the hospital had its genesis back in 1971 when an agreement was reached between the Commonwealth Government and the Little Company of Mary to construct and operate a public hospital with up to 300 beds to service the inner north and Belconnen districts. It was agreed that the hospital would be built in the recently founded suburb of Bruce. That agreement predated the ACT Government by about 17 years and ultimately led to some confusion over the ownership of the hospital.

In 2009, with the ACT hospital system reaching capacity, the ACT Government investigated bringing Calvary Hospital under full government ownership and control. The Government was concerned about paying to upgrade a hospital which it then believed it did not own.

The Little Company of Mary reached in-principle agreement with the Government to relinquish its lease in return for $77 million. Only after agreement was reached did the Catholic Archbishop of Canberra and Goulburn, Mark Coleridge, publicly state his opposition to the deal. It is likely the board would not have begun negotiations had the Archbishop's position been known at the outset. Though his opposition might have ultimately been overcome, it would probably have delayed the sale for years, which was not acceptable to the board or the Government.

So the board withdrew from the hospital transaction in February 2010. In 2009 its chairman, Tom Brennan, had said that failure to sell the hospital to the ACT Government would probably lead to the collapse of the Calvary public and private hospitals at Bruce within a year or two.

That outcome was averted, but not without much stress on Brennan and ACT Health Minister Katy Gallagher. In retrospect, it might have been better for all if the proposal for the Government to purchase the hospital had never been put.

There was considerable public opposition, firstly because critics felt that the Little Company of Mary Health Care should not be paid $77 million for a hospital it had not paid to build. Secondly, the agreement in principle to sell Calvary Hospital included an arrangement for the Little Company of Mary to buy Canberra's hospice, Clare Holland House, which it already operated. The Palliative Care Society was concerned that privatisation of ownership would result in deterioration of palliative care, that contrary to Brennan's assurances it would lead to the imposition of Catholic values on patients. Also volunteers felt that their direct involvement at the hospice would diminish.

Mackay, who was not directly involved in the negotiations, believed the board made two fundamental mistakes, the first of which was the decision to include the hospice in the deal.

"We just created a second enemy on another flank while we were trying to do the main deal." Supporters of Clare Holland House ran a highly successful campaign against the sale of the hospice and, according to Mackay, "ran interference like you wouldn't believe. They were very, very effective— far more effective than we were in countering them."

Secondly, Archbishop Coleridge was not treated with due respect early in the process. Although it would have been difficult to get him onside, his opposition to the sale made negotiations much more difficult and protracted than was necessary. During that time the ACT Government received legal advice that it owned the hospital and that it could not buy something it already owned. The Little Company of Mary had legal advice that it owned the hospital. But the Government's advice was sufficient to sink the deal because no agreement could be reached.

"I sat through board meetings and committee meetings after committee meetings trying to find a way through but I don't think we were ever going to, once we had made those two fundamental mistakes." On one occasion, Mackay was able to arrange a meeting in his lounge room on a Saturday morning, with Brennan, Stanhope and Gallagher. "We tried to cut a deal. But that went nowhere."

At least, after all of the frustration on both sides, the result was an arrangement that he believes is better than anything Calvary had in the past. "We now have peace in our time."

Previously the hospital's relationship with bureaucrats had not been productive. Successive CEOs could not stay for long because it was too frustrating. Finally, a good relationship was established between the hospital management and the ACT Health Department and between the chair of the Little Company of Mary Health care, John Watkins, and ACT Chief Minister Katy Gallagher. Despite all of the frustration, Mackay says "my time with the Little Company of Mary has been one of the great parts of my life."

The board of CIC Australia is one of the many others he has served on. CIC Australia began in Canberra in 1986 under the name Jerrabomberra Estates. It has developed about ten Canberra suburbs and major urban projects around Australia. In 2013, when Peet Limited purchased a controlling interest in CIC in the Australian Stock Exchange, Mackay was the only non-executive director to remain on the board.

Another board position was with Australian Satellite Communications, which began in 1985, providing satellite services to remote areas in Australia. It uses satellites to provide communication links. The business has spread to the Pacific and has developed other commercial communication services around Australia. It is now owned by global company SpeedCast, based in Hong Kong, of which Mackay has become chairman.

Datapod, which began in Australia and now operates internationally, builds modular data centres and is another firm with John Mackay on its board. Other board positions have been with organisations that provide services to people who are disadvantaged.

Mackay's membership of boards was not limited to major commercial ventures. Indeed, he has frequently been attracted to or sought by boards of organisations that provide services to people who are disadvantaged in one way or another.

John helps direct organisations such as the Ricky Stuart Foundation, which aims to increase understanding of autism, support the care of autistic people and provide respite for supporting families.

Ricky Stuart, a former player and coach with the Canberra Raiders Rugby League team, has a daughter with autism. He said the care and special services a family needs to help support a loved one can be financially and mentally draining.

Even with membership of up to eight boards, some of which include subcommittees, John seemed to have little difficulty in finding enough time for a fairly hectic social life. He attributed this to his being highly organised and a good manager of time: "I am absolutely focused on outcome. I don't

Paul Walshe, marketing manager at ActewAGL, looks understandably nervous sitting next to John, pink-clad, at Albert Hall in Canberra for the annual Pink Dinner, preparing to auction the handbag for charity, in 2008.

mind hard work—I never have—and if I have too much to do I don't mind losing a bit of sleep."

When required, including in early days at ACTEW, he would frequently begin work at about 4 a.m. and work until about 6 p.m. He normally managed with four to five hours sleep at night but frequently had a 15 minute siesta. "I had this view that if I had a couple of hours start on the rest of the field, most days of my life I was going to be more successful than most of the field."

Mackay's positive leadership and management capacity are widely recognised. At his farewell as CEO of ActewAGL, chairman Jim Service said one of the finest advantages and the greatest piece of good luck he had as chairman was having Mackay as the CEO during almost the entire time he was chairman.

He praised Mackay's re-emphasis on the safety of staff: "We want them to go home safely every night. John has improved the safety performance enormously and that reflects his care about people. So, I was terribly lucky. I was able to sit back, pat John on the back for doing good things and even get the backwash of some of the quality."

Mackay's commitment to safety was strengthened by the death of two linesmen soon after his appointment to ACTEW. He had to tell one man's wife her husband would not come home. "That experience will live with me for ever."

He has frequently spoken to various groups about leadership which he said he learned from Scouts, cadets, university, from some great bosses, some shocking bosses and "by learning every time you make a mistake."

He says the basics of his leadership were simple:
* a clear set of goals that could be understood by all and the achievement of which could easily be measured

- a mapped out journey and an ability to explain simply where the organisation was on the journey
- a simple record of agreed actions, responsibilities and progress
- treating staff like family and communicating regularly with them
- a great senior management team with varying approaches and skills
- delegation of authority and clear accountability
- financial incentives paid on a group basis, and
- speedy and simplified decision making processes.

The focus on success operated in parallel with a strenuous social life. Long lunches and evening functions about five nights a week were typical. It was not uncommon for Mackay to attend several cocktail functions in one evening and he could not be correctly described as a moderate drinker.

He tried to fit in a game of golf at least once a week, more for the social contact than for the game itself. "I tend to do a lot of networking, especially with my regular golfing partners such as Hawkie [Allan Hawke], Brian Acworth, Paul Herrick, Ian Hansen, Kieran Gilbert and Terry Weber. We tell shocking jokes and do a fair bit of sledging. But we also exchange a lot of information and ideas."

He never bothered to have much contact with the Canberra diplomatic set. But when participating in a special golf day for ambassadors and local business leaders, he made a great friend of the US Ambassador Jeffery Bliech. They had regular contact off the golf course. John and Colette attended an intimate Thanksgiving Day dinner with Jeff and Bekky Bliech in November 2012.

John also befriended the Chilean Ambassador Pedro Pablo Diaz, a former head of Coca-Cola for South America. They played regular golf games, and John worked with him to help solve problems and to open doors for him. John helped him to arrange the installation of a special public art project in Canberra's Latin American Plaza, west of Civic.

The installation is a capsule that was used to rescue the 33 Chilean miners trapped underground for 69 days when the Copiapó mine collapsed in 2010.

John was delighted to be awarded the Grande Order of Bernardo O'Higgins by the President of Chile in 2012. It is the highest award to a non-citizen of Chile and the first to be awarded to an Australian for a decade.

Other forms of recreation that have attracted Mackay include racehorses. For some 15 years, as a member of the Carbine club, he owned shares in various race horses. Some have been winners, but he has generally viewed horse racing as a social pastime.

He insisted on calling one of the horses in which he had an interest "Gilded Youth". The name reflects his love of Banjo Paterson's poetry. "The Man from Ironbark" supplied the inspiration:

There were some gilded youths that sat along the barber's wall.

Their eyes were dull, their heads were flat, they had no brains at all;

As it turned out, Gilded Youth was more successful than others in which Mackay had an interest and earned its owners $375,000. He says while this sounds like a lot it has to be balanced against the expense of feeding and training horses: "We probably made no dough out of it whatsoever."

Racehorses provided a ticket for fun. He did not apply the same business principles to investment in racehorses as when sitting on a corporate board. Most were bought after extremely long lunches.

"Well, you would have to put the social benefits in to make it into a winner. Racing is all about being king for the day. Whether you take your horse to Flemington or to Boggabri—the thing wins, you will cheer, you will get on the grog and you have usually taken some bookie for a ride."

He doesn't take a regular interest in horse racing. He only gets involved when a horse he has a share in is racing. Essentially, investment in horse racing is about having a good time with mates, and networking. "Like almost everything I do, it is good fun with a regular healthy dash of alcohol."

In March 2011, John Mackay was inducted as Chancellor of the University of Canberra. He had previously been asked to join the university's council but had no real interest at that time. He certainly had no interest in further formal study.

His interest in the university was reignited during its 40th anniversary commemorations, particularly as he participated in the packing of a time capsule. The Chancellor Ingrid Moses encouraged him to join the council so he could be her replacement. "Sitting in a boring council meeting had no appeal to me whatsoever. But running the place had a lot more appeal." After attending only a couple of council meetings he was unanimously elected chancellor for three years.

He found those three years most interesting and rewarding. During that time the university took several major initiatives and greatly enhanced its reputation. John insists that the credit was due almost entirely to Vice-Chancellor Stephen Parker, whom he describes as a star.

Professor Parker began as the Vice-Chancellor on 1 March 2007. He had previously been the Senior Deputy Vice-Chancellor at Monash University in Melbourne. Mackay particularly appreciated Parker's enthusiasm, lateral thinking and entrepreneurial approach to the life of the university. Mackay, with similar characteristics, saw his role as clearing pathways for Parker's ideas.

These included a suggestion by Parker that the university become the major sponsor of the Canberra Brumbies Rugby Union team. Then came the

How the future unfolds: John's official portrait as retiring Chancellor of the University of Canberra in 2013, holding a photograph of the young John Mackay graduating from the same university some 35 years earlier. (Picture by William Hall)

establishment of a hospital and a GP super-clinic as well as the building of a 500 bed student residence.

Meanwhile, Mackay introduced several influential friends and colleagues to the management of the university: "Since I have been there, probably coincidentally, the university has gone gangbusters." By the time of Mackay's resignation as Chancellor, the university was in the best shape it had been since its foundation. The key measurements were at their highest: student numbers, student satisfaction, research funding, and publications. The university that year posted a record surplus. In the QS World Rankings, the University of Canberra was in the top five per cent of universities around the world.

Surveys showed that University of Canberra graduates were among the highest paid and most employable in Australia. The university had developed additional accommodation and teaching facilities. A health complex was added, a new sporting complex was being developed and a deal was signed to build a public hospital on the campus. And against trends at most other Australian universities, the number of international students at the University of Canberra continued to grow.

Mackay was confident that the university would become effectively a suburb in its own right: "All of the spare land we have will eventually be taken up by things which make us money."

Despite considerable financial pressure on Australian universities generally, the University of Canberra was, toward the end of Mackay's three-year term as chancellor, better off financially than it had ever been.

"I have noticed the status of our university increase very substantially. Again I take no credit for that in a personal sense but I do take some credit for running the board of the university in a way that would enable that to happen." He was particularly proud to be replaced as chancellor at the end of his three-year term by Dr Tom Calma, one of the few indigenous Australians in senior governance positions in higher education and at the time of writing the only indigenous chancellor in Australia. Dr Calma, previously the university's deputy chancellor, was the 2013 ACT Australian of the Year.

The University of Canberra awarded degrees twice yearly in the Great Hall of Parliament House. This was not something Mackay looked forward to. He was constantly concerned that women in high heels would trip and fall or he would look the wrong way when photographs were taken. Nevertheless, he enjoyed these formal occasions once they were under way. "It is a really inspirational day to see so many bright young people ready to take on the world, armed with a UC education."

At a University of Canberra dinner in 2012, with Bryce Courtenay.

18

MARSHALLING RESOURCES TO SERVE THE DISABLED

Soon after the establishment of ActewAGL, ACT Deputy Chief Minister Ted Quinlan asked John Mackay to join the board of Koomarri, which provides residential services and supported employment to disabled people. Quinlan, who many years earlier was head of the ACT Electricity Authority, was, when he approached John, the domestic partner of Koomarri's CEO, Margaret Spalding. He said the board lacked leadership and John could help Margaret Spalding by joining. On the board, John found that other members of the board understood disability well and were passionate about the role of Koomarri, but lacked business experience and the ability to attract outside support.

As Quinlan no doubt knew, John was blessed with both attributes. He could also direct some of ActewAGL's resources to Koomarri when required.

Margaret Spalding, who had already steered Koomarri through several crises, made an immediate impression on Mackay as a highly dedicated, intelligent and well-regarded woman. "We became really, really good mates very, very quickly."

After a few board meetings Mackay determined, with encouragement from Spalding, to become chair of the board. Having done so, he encouraged people with good management skills to join the board. These included James Service (son of Jim Service) and Len Early, the former Deputy Secretary of the Finance Department. Service took over as chairman after Mackay left and Early as treasurer.

Koomarri at that time operated from a former warehouse in the industrial suburb of Fyshwick, surrounded by car dealers and brothels. Its finances were stretched to the limit and, as Mackay found when he could not send an email to Spalding, the IT system was on its knees.

So Mackay sent senior members of the IT team from ActewAGL to Koomarri with the instruction that they were not to return until Koomarri had a fully functioning IT system. Similarly, when Spalding wanted tables, chairs and marquees for a Christmas party, Mackay simply instructed his staff to arrange it. "I could do things like that without any trouble at all."

The complete unsuitability of the Koomarri building in Fyshwick and its location were obvious on first going in. They were obvious too to Margaret Spalding, who it turned out could sometimes be a real schemer. She decided that among other committees there should be a property committee. Mackay agreed to chair it, not immediately aware that this was her code for "Let's have a new building." So plans began for a new HQ for Koomarri.

Koomarri's other properties included Cut Cloth in Belconnen, Easy Iron in Braddon, a couple of opportunity shops and a gardening business. More significant was a caravan park in Narrabundah that would become a catalyst for a major upheaval in Koomarri and arguably at least contributed to Margaret Spalding's untimely death.

Initially, however, the need for a new headquarters was the focus for the property committee. Mackay, with ready access to senior ACT public servants, arranged an appointment for himself and Spalding with the CEO of the ACT Land Development Agency, which allocated to Koomarri a block of land in Phillip.

Although Koomarri had existed in Canberra for many years and had earned its reputation for doing good, the extent and nature of its services were not well known. Mackay arranged to have a video made to illustrate the services it provided and to explain its need for a new headquarters building.

"I then put one of our ACTEW tents on the [Phillip] site and I invited the top end of town to come for a presentation on Koomarri." By then, architect Rodney Moss had prepared sketches of the proposed building. After speeches by Mackay and Spalding, the invited guests made numerous offers of services or cash to help the project.

Canberra airport, for example, donated the same type of carpet as was being used at its new terminal. Goods such as toilets and tiles were donated and Paul Murphy of Project Co-ordination offered to manage the project at no charge. James Service committed his consultancy JG Service Pty Ltd to oversee the project for one dollar. It soon became clear the building, costing some $2 million, could be constructed for less than $1 million after donations. Within a remarkably short time, construction was well underway. It all seemed too good to be true.

In a way it was. Early one morning James Service rang to say that some bastard had burned the half built structure to the ground. "I was almost speechless as I got in my car to drive over there. This had been my baby and I was showing how I could deliver miracles with a bit of help from my friends."

With typically positive thinking, before he even reached the building Mackay had decided to turn disaster into opportunity: "In no time at all we had money flowing in." So much money flowed in that about an extra $500,000 supplemented the insurance payment. The numerous offers of help had included a fund raising garden party at Government House in Yarralumla.

But as John drove to inspect the damage, he was agonising over how he could arrange to watch his horse, Gilded Youth, run that afternoon in Sydney. Coincidentally, James Service had a horse running in the same race.

First, he had to console tearful staff and the tradespeople who had lost all their tools in the fire. Even as he spoke to the media, he still had ambitions of catching the 11 a.m. flight to Sydney. He did, accompanied by Service. They took a taxi to Randwick and arrived in time to see the race. Was it worth the effort? "Well, mine beat his but something else beat both of them."

Many phone calls came in during the hurry to watch the race. John hesitated to take one of the calls, from someone who had been plaguing him over recent weeks about a business proposal, but decided he must. He told the caller, known for his lengthy phone calls, that unless it could be quick he would have to call back. The caller said it was quick: he was simply offering $50,000 for the rebuilding.

Later, well aware of the tedium and poor food often associated with fundraising dinners, Mackay decided to stage a practical joke. He sent out invitations to an expensive dinner to be held in the worst possible venue at the most inconvenient time: the Soldiers Club Hall at Yass on Christmas Eve. The cost would be $2500 for a table of ten, with 47 items to be auctioned and speeches by at least three people.

Invitees were given the option of not attending as long as they paid for a table: "I sold 20 tables but one person thought it was real and was going to come anyway."

Ultimately, the new building was opened by the Chief Minister Jon Stanhope, with the band of the Royal Military College, Duntroon. Many clients of Koomarri were present, as were the generous benefactors who supported the project.

The joy of triumph can be shortlived. The success and happiness generated by that day were soon soured by the sale of the caravan park that had been bought by Koomarri from the ACT Government for $1 in 2001. Previously the park had been run by a government agency and it was transferred to Koomarri on condition that the organisation would continue to operate it as a caravan park for at least five years.

Whether or not the true state of the park was known to Koomarri when it took over is not clear. But it was not operating as a normal caravan park. Most, perhaps all, of its residents had virtual permanent tenure. Most had rent arrears and many had installed unapproved structures to extend their immobile caravans. The initial hope that some of Koomarri's disabled clients would be employed at the caravan park proved baseless. Instead of being an asset, the park proved a liability to Koomarri.

"We had an absolute nightmare trying to get people to pay their rent or getting them out when they didn't. So effectively we had this complete dog on our hands which we felt had some value."

The first attempt at realising this potential value was to draw up leases which made it clear the residents did not have tenure and that they could be evicted for non-payment of rent. But the residents refused to sign. So, as the required five years had passed, the board decided to sell the caravan park.

Koomarri sought expressions of interest and the board believed an offer of $2 million from a developer, Consolidated Builders was too good to refuse. It was about $600,000 more than the next best offer, and the sale was completed in March 2006.

The ink had barely dried on the contract before the company sent eviction notices to the tenants, about 100 in all. After public concern, the eviction notices were stayed while the Government and the developer negotiated to secure a future for the tenants.

Koomarri was criticised for profiting without reasonable care for the tenants. In hindsight Mackay realised that the intentions of the developer might have been foreseen, but he said that at no time had Koomarri known of the developer's plans.

Although it was the developer that issued the eviction notices the damage to Koomarri's reputation was significant. In less than two weeks, a meeting was held that included Chief Minister Stanhope, Mackay, Spalding and the managing director of Consolidated Builders, Josip Zivko, to seek a solution.

With Spalding in tears and Stanhope nonplussed, Mackay offered to return the purchase price and for Koomarri to take back the caravan park. Zivko, almost entirely insulated from the public criticism, and apparently with no care for the reputation of Koomarri, refused the offer.

Ultimately the ACT Government arranged a land swap with Zivko and resumed the caravan park. Koomarri paid almost half the money it had received for the sale to the Government as compensation. The developer was the only party of the three not to lose from the settlement. "I just thought his act was appalling," Mackay said. "We were naive and stupid to think of dealing with someone like him—we should have known better."

Margaret Spalding's reputation for her dedication to Koomarri and its clients was beyond question. Neither was it her decision to sell the caravan park to this particular developer. Negotiations for the sale were handled by a committee of the board, which sent instructions to a lawyer for the transaction. Believing she had been branded a liar by Mike Jeffreys on Canberra radio station 2CC in 2006, she took defamation action against him. During the hearings, only days before her death, she described hearing herself called a liar as like "having my guts torn out".

One of Margaret Spalding's sons rang John on 24 March 2004 just as he was leaving Canberra Airport on his way home from Sydney, with the news that she had taken her own life. "I had to ask him three times just to make sure I had not misheard him. I went off with a very heavy heart and helped to arrange her funeral which I made sure was a great celebration of her life."

Several weeks previously, in a conversation in her office, Margaret had told Mackay she had put together a very good team at Koomarri and that if she disappeared the team would be fine. John believes that her death was a great loss to Canberra and to the disabled people she served. The ACT coroner found there were no suspicious circumstances. She was due to receive a Medal of the Order of Australia (OAM) for her contribution to the disability services sector, later that year.

Whether her death was directly or entirely because of the defamation action cannot be known. Mackay insists that neither Spalding nor he had any idea of Zivko's intentions before the caravan park was sold. "I didn't know Zivko from a bar of soap. Had I known him I would not have sold it to him. But I had no idea what he would do."

Though he had advised Spalding not to take legal action against Jeffreys and 2CC, Mackay regretted not having given this advice more strongly. During the turmoil after the sale, he handled most of the media inquiries, specifically to protect Spalding.

Before he left the board of Koomarri, after about ten years' service, the organisation's Belconnen workshop was named the John Mackay Building. The auspicious day on which the building was named began with his participation in a torch relay for the 2008 Olympic Games.

John left his car at a sister-in-law's house in Ainslie and rode his bicycle from there to Commonwealth Avenue, where his leg of the relay began. Having completed that section of the relay, he rode his bicycle back to Ainslie.

With grandson Jack Cassidy at the launch of the John Mackay Building at Koomarri, by Thérèse Rein, wife of Prime Minister Kevin Rudd. (Picture by Lyn Mills)

There he changed into a suit and drove to Belconnen, where the building was opened by Thérèse Rein, wife of Prime Minister Kevin Rudd, who had previously worked for Koomarri. John was deeply touched by the occasion.

Some months later a neighbour got in touch to say there had been a burglary and suggested checking to see whether anything was missing. There was—John's bicycle. The neighbour, it happened, had seen what he believed to be Mackay's bicycle being ridden through Civic. He had even considered approaching the felon riding the machine but thought better of it. Later still, John's sister-in-law rang, wanting to know when he was going to pick up the bicycle he had left at her Ainslie house on the day of the torch relay.

19

HOW TO CATCH A SEA LION WITHOUT EVEN TRYING

John Mackay was a child of the inland, but the sea offered some of his greatest pleasures and an ideal retreat from meetings and civic responsibilities. He hasn't always accorded the sea the respect it demands and, as on the road, has paid a price for thumbing his nose at rules intended to keep people safe.

This affinity began in the early 1970s. John, Colette and baby Jane drove to the New South Wales south coast. The journey along the notoriously dangerous Kings Highway, is taken by tens of thousands of Canberrans seeking relief from inland summer heat. It is locally said that almost everyone in Canberra heads for the coast to get away from everyone else in Canberra.

Colette's parents, Rex and Deirdre, owned a caravan in the Broulee Beach Caravan Park. On that first journey they shared the caravan with Colette's parents and about five of her brothers and sisters.

The park, adequate but basic, had a central amenities block and a laundry and accommodated about 50 other caravans. It was close to beautiful Broulee Beach, which is protected at one end by a headland and island and extends about seven kilometres south to the Moruya River. Despite the somewhat cramped accommodation, their first trip as a family to Broulee introduced John and Colette to the beauty, serenity and fun offered by the coast.

Shortly afterwards, when Rex was promoted to head Customs in New South Wales, he moved the caravan to the Central Coast. John and Colette visited only once. The caravan was crowded with eight occupants including Jane in nappies. High winds blew and torrential rain fell. Undaunted, John and Rex went beach fishing every day. But when John noticed Colette's frustration the visit ended, not before he entertained everyone in the communal laundry as he attempted to wash nappies while Colette was at church.

After Rex was transferred to Melbourne, John returned the caravan to Broulee, where he and his family often had weekends and holidays over the next 20 years. Improvements and additions included a telephone and fax—it was the only caravan so well equipped for keeping in touch with Canberra.

Broulee became a second home. John and Colette grew closer to Colette's sister, Margaret, and her husband, Ian. They shared the accommodation, boat, child minding and party convening. On most nights, there was a fire set in an old washing machine tub and a meal was prepared outside for numerous guests. Frequently, about 20 people shared dinner, many of them gathered by John and Ian while fishing or rambling along the beach.

As at home in Canberra, alcohol was plentiful. The children on holiday enjoyed relative freedom from parental control. For the adults regular golf and card games contributed to the fun and laughter.

Once after a big party, John and Ian found themselves with a large group of mates playing a rough game of tackle-frisbee. It was well after midnight when John thought he spotted Ian swimming in fairly large surf quite a way from shore. He swam out to bring him in but no one was there because Ian was still sitting on the beach. After John eventually got to bed he was woken by Colette angrily thumping on his back. He had gone to bed without washing off, and a lot of the Broulee sand had come back with him.

New friends included the Perkins and Dye families. Within a week of meeting David Perkins and going fishing in his boat, John bought a boat of his own. He became one of the most successful snapper fishermen in the district. For more than 40 years, offshore fishing with mates, son Ben and father-in-law Rex became almost an obsession. It was rare for him to return without a spectacular catch which he and Colette would cook to perfection.

Fishing adventures took him to most parts of Australia. Once, about 40 kilometres off the Queensland coast, he landed a 320 kilogram black marlin, which he tagged and released.

Part of the routine when going fishing was taking care not to leave the bait in the freezer—normally a sound procedure except for the night before a particular trip, when he put the frozen bait into the boat, but found next morning the local cats had beaten him to it.

Another time he left a sinker on the ground at the Broulee Caravan Park attached to the line of his rod that was in the back of the boat. On arrival at the Mossy Point boat ramp two kilometres away there was smoke coming from the fishing reel and 500 metres of fishing line was unravelled somewhere on the road behind him.

John fancied his navigation skills, which were tested one morning when, in thick fog, he headed for Montague Island, about nine kilometres off Narooma. His companions were reluctant to go through the notoriously dangerous bar, let alone have Mackay try for the island with no compass.

He assured them he could find the island with his eyes closed and ploughed ahead. After travelling for rather too long, the crew completely lost confidence but captain Mackay insisted all was well. There was almost a mutiny, but finally he declared some success as some large rocks loomed out of the gloom. He was severely mocked for many months after the fog lifted. They had travelled in a circle some 25 kilometres in circumference and were almost back where they started.

In early days at the coast, John used to dive for abalone. There was always a party for the delicate preparation, cooking and eating of the abalone. He became a proficient scuba diver. On his first dive he recklessly went down to about 30 metres, in a sea lion colony at Montague Island. His lack of any formal training and licence to dive was no inhibitor.

John drove a boat for about 30 years without a licence. That came to an end when, returning to shore with son Ben driving, Mackay encouraged his offspring not to be fussed about the requirement to reduce speed or wearing a life jacket as they approached the land. When ordered to stop by a maritime inspector, he insisted he was responsible for the boat but his attempt to have his son exonerated failed. With complete evenhandedness, the authorities fined each of them $1,000.

Sea voyages with friends involved far more than fishing. Almost every time they saw something special or had an adventure. These have included whales surfacing nearby and hooking a large shark. And there are remarkable stories of the one that got away. Alcohol and the passage of time inevitably enlarged the uncaught prey in campfire recollections and in later years.

One day Rex was fishing with John on a reef about 15 kilometres southeast of home. They already had a boatload of nice snapper when all four lines went off at once. After a scramble, three more snapper joined the catch. Then John grabbed Rex's rod to pull in what he believed to be a tiddler. They were in 80 metres of water and the fish was almost on the bottom. Suddenly, the rod was almost pulled from his hands.

The two men took 15 minutes to get the fish to about 20 metres below the boat. Then it took off horizontally at top speed. Finally a huge sea lion surfaced, more than 100 metres from the boat, with a 12 kilogram kingfish

The one that almost got away: the kingfish rescued from the jaws of the sea lion, pictured with its two captors.

in its mouth, still on the line, They chased the sea lion and John belted it with a paddle and retrieved the kingfish with a gaff. The sea lion was not amused and was preparing to leap aboard and retrieve its meal when John started the boat and got away at high speed.

Absorbed by the pursuit of the sea lion, the intrepid anglers paid no attention to the developing storm. By the time they reached safety, they were drenched and almost exhausted.

Only when cleaning the kingfish did they realise why John initially believed he'd caught a tiddler: there it was in the gut of the kingfish, still with the hook in its mouth—a tiny example of the food chain in action.

John has even managed to let fish get away after landing them successfully. There was one beauty he held over the side to clean, having removed the hook from its mouth. The slippery fish might have heard loud curses as it made its bid for freedom and swam away.

It's not only fish that have got away. Two mobile phones and several fishing rods have joined many knives and cutting boards in the waters of the Pacific.

In the late 1990s, the Mackays moved out of the caravan park and bought a small cottage in Broulee, which became the venue for many parties over the next seven years. Then they built a beautiful house with stunning ocean views at nearby Mossy Point.

Colette, John and the family, including Colette's parents, go to the coast house for Christmas every year and rarely return until late January. The holiday house has plenty of room for parties. It can accommodate all the children and grandchildren, who visit regularly, as well as Colette's extended family, who use the downstairs flat. Dinner parties for more than 20 are common.

20

LEAVING ACTEWAGL AFTER 15 YEARS

With about 50 per cent of its population working in the public service, Canberra is effectively a company town. Whereas in most cities and towns it is considered impolite to ask what one's neighbours or friends are paid, such information is generally known or easily obtained for public servants because pay rates are set based on the level at which they work.

ACTEW employees are not technically public servants, because ACTEW is a territory-owned corporation. ACTEW staff, especially at senior levels, are engaged on contracts with agreed salaries set by the corporation's board. Nevertheless, there is something of a perception in Canberra that people have the right to know what senior managers of major corporations are paid. The information was for many years not made public by ACTEW, but a change to legislation in 2010 required ACTEW to include it in annual reports.

Shortly before this change, there was considerable political and media curiosity about the salary of ACTEW managing director Mark Sullivan. John Mackay, as chairman of the ACTEW board, telephoned the author, then a journalist on *The Canberra Times*, with the relevant information and the newspaper reported Sullivan's annual salary as $621,171. That produced barely a flicker of public or political interest. Yet the misreporting of Sullivan's salary in the subsequent annual report was the catalyst for Mackay's resignation.

The error was not his nor, apparently, was it noticed by anyone for more than 12 months. Ultimately it was difficult to understand whether the political and public outrage over the under-reporting of Sullivan's salary was driven more by envy over the level of his salary than by the error.

While the 2011 annual report was being prepared, the shareholders, ACT Treasurer Andrew Barr and Chief Minister Katy Gallagher, asked for details of Sullivan's salary. Mackay asked the company secretary for the relevant information, which came from material being prepared for the 2010/11 annual report. They decided to send a letter with the details to the shareholders. That letter was signed by Mackay and sent shortly before the annual report was tabled in the Legislative Assembly.

The report was issued to the shareholders on 16 September 2011. Like most annual reports, this one attracted little interest.

On 24 September the following year, the 2011/12 annual report was issued and, like its predecessor, at first caused no controversy.

The first indication that something was wrong came less than two weeks later, on 3 October, when ACTEW's company secretary noticed an inconsistency in the figures on Sullivan's salary in the successive annual reports. On the same day it was confirmed that the 2010/11 report and the letter to the shareholders in 2011 both said Sullivan's remuneration package was $621,171. The correct figure had been $855,588.

How or why the error occurred is not known. According to Mackay, "It was just a straight out stuff up." Apparently someone in ACTEW's human resources section failed to include Sullivan's incentive payments in the figure published in 2010/11.

Given that the error had been effectively corrected in the more recent report, there might well have been an argument for letting sleeping dogs lie. Instead, and no doubt correctly, on the day the company secretary informed Mackay and Sullivan of the error, they instructed the secretary to take appropriate action to correct the error. Six days later the secretary sought external legal advice on issuing a corrigendum. The relevant legislation gave no guidance on what to do over a year after publishing an error.

On 30 October, ten days after the 2012 ACT election, the ACTEW company secretary received legal advice recommending contact with the Chief Minister and Cabinet Directorate to determine the level of publication or notification required.

The new Legislative Assembly first sat on 6 November 2012 and Katy Gallagher was re-elected as Chief Minister. On 9 November, the ACTEW company secretary telephoned the Chief Minister and Cabinet Directorate and was advised to send an email about issuing a corrigendum. This was done the same day. After receiving no reply, the secretary sent a follow up email on 27 November. Having still received no reply by 14 December, the secretary had a telephone discussion with the Commissioner for Public Administration, Andrew Kefford, who said there had been no advice or contact from Chief Minister and Cabinet Directorate officers. Kefford said a letter and corrigendum should be prepared and sent to the Treasurer and thence forwarded to the Speaker of the assembly.

The requested material was sent promptly to the Cabinet Directorate but went no further while staff waited for legal advice on the question of the elapsed time and the issuing of a corrigendum. On 18 January 2013, the ACTEW company secretary sought a meeting with senior directorate officers to discuss, among other matters, the outstanding advice on a corrigendum. A meeting was held on 23 January, at which stage the Directorate had still received no legal advice on how the matter should be handled.

It seems that meeting at least prompted a response on the following day, confirming that legislation and annual report directions gave little guidance. But the officer thought it was worth issuing a corrigendum. So it can be seen that the Directorate took almost 11 weeks to come up with a fairly vague response to the question first put by ACTEW's company secretary on 9 November 2012.

ACTEW then spoke with its auditors and on 4 March the company secretary advised Mackay that a letter and corrigendum would be prepared for Mackay to send to the ACT Treasurer, Andrew Barr. This was done on 8 March.

Mackay met with Barr and Gallagher ten days later. Katy Gallagher, on the same day, wrote to Mackay seeking information and clarification on how the error had occurred and he replied that day. On the following day, 19 March, Andrew Barr tabled the corrigendum in the Legislative Assembly. Also on that day, Gallagher and Barr wrote again to Mackay seeking more information on how the error had occurred.

Though Barr later acknowledged that the correct figure had been published in the subsequent annual report, he told the Legislative Assembly he was surprised and disappointed by the discrepancy.

The ACTEW board discussed the matter on March 20 and on the following day Mackay wrote to Barr and Gallagher, providing more information and a chronology of events. They wrote again on 25 March requesting even more information and he replied on 28 March. This followed a special board meeting the previous day.

By then the matter was receiving wide media coverage which focussed not only on the error in the 2011 report but on how much Mark Sullivan was being paid.

During the flurry of publicity, Sullivan offered to take a pay cut of $141,000. Gallagher rejected the offer, saying it was not her job even to consider the offer. She said it was the role of the ACTEW board to set Sullivan's salary but she had asked for reassurance that the managing director's pay level was appropriate.

At the ACTEW board meeting of 15 April, Mackay announced that he would resign as chairman of ACTEW and ActewAGL from 30 June 2013.

Of course, in hindsight, it is easy for critics to point an accusing finger at the board, at Mackay as chairman, or at Sullivan, for failing to recognise the error. It might be just as easy to ask why shareholders Barr and Gallagher, having supported the legislation to require the general manager's salary to be disclosed, did not question the boosted figure in the 2012 annual report. But as Mackay said, most board members were not expected to pore over annual reports to ensure that every figure was correct.

In contrast to the bureaucratic delay while ACTEW sought advice from the Chief Minister and Cabinet Directorate, Mackay received a prompt response from Gallagher and Barr after he wrote to advise them of the error. He was requested to attend a meeting with the Chief Minister and Treasurer and did so, fully expecting a calm conversation over the cause of the error and the appropriate action to be taken.

"I walked in and Katy was visibly angry—very angry." First, the politicians told him that the error been made at a time when ACTEW was under pressure to provide details of Sullivan's salary. In his defence, Mackay pointed out that, had there been a conspiracy to mislead anyone over Sullivan's salary, it would not have been detailed correctly in the following annual report.

Secondly, Gallagher wanted to know how the board could justify paying Sullivan so much money. Mackay responded by explaining that the salary was benchmarked against the remuneration received by people with similar responsibilities and that it was a salary comparable with the amount that Sullivan would have received had he remained as head of a major government department.

At that time, as managing director of ACTEW, Sullivan was responsible for the everyday supply of water and sewerage services to Canberra, for the construction of a pipeline between the Murrumbidgee River and Googong Dam, and for the construction of the enlarged Cotter Dam. The value of these projects was well over $600 million. These projects were the most significant capital works in Canberra since the construction of Parliament House in the 1980s. As well as these projects, Sullivan had very significant responsibilities as a director on the boards of ActewAGL, TransACT and Ecowise Environmental.

Mackay's justification of Sullivan's salary received little sympathy from the Chief Minister, who noted that her salary was far less. She was also angry about the time taken to notify her and the Treasurer of the error. Naturally, Mackay pointed out that her senior bureaucrats had been made aware of the error several months earlier and had apparently not considered it serious enough to tell her.

Mackay considered he was on firm ground, not least because Sullivan's salary had been negotiated by the previous chairman, Jim Service, and had been endorsed by the entire ACTEW board. Further, ACTEW had identified the incorrect figure and had taken steps to have the error corrected.

This was not the first time Gallagher had raised concerns about ACTEW, ActewAGL or Mackay. He had received informal advice that she believed he had not shown her due respect at a meeting: "I thought to myself, that is not correct, and I took no notice of it," Mackay said.

Perhaps he should have taken notice. On reflection he said that the perceived slight "was going on as a subtext and I think the salary stuff, rightly or wrongly, significantly threw fuel on the fire."

The meeting ended with the Chief Minister telling Mackay that she was going to write him a letter. It duly arrived, replete with blunt questions on how seriously he took his responsibility as chairman of ACTEW. "I believe someone in her office was helping her out in dealing with this matter. There was this general concern that we were out of control and possibly that I was not treating her with sufficient respect. And once this stuff got legs in the media you had a perfect storm."

It seems likely much of the information supplied to the media, particularly to The Canberra Times and the ABC, came directly or indirectly from Gallagher's office.

Whatever the rights and wrongs of any difference between Mackay and Gallagher, there is no doubt the error over Sullivan's salary greatly inflamed the situation. The public row that erupted, though initially focusing on the under-reporting of Sullivan's salary in the previous annual report, quickly moved to a debate over whether Sullivan should be paid as much as he was being paid. In her public comments, Gallagher made it clear she believed the salary was excessive.

Since the establishment of ActewAGL in October 2000 as a joint venture between ACTEW and AGL, there has been general public confusion between the two. It seems this confusion extended even to the Chief Minister.

One of her concerns was that ActewAGL, had paid about $70,000 for a suite at the Derby in Melbourne. It must be remembered ActewAGL, as opposed to ACTEW itself, was a commercial venture and as such was entitled to make commercial decisions. Further, as Mackay explained to Gallagher, most of the tables in that suite were sublet to other commercial organisations, including ACTTAB, also then a territory-owned corporation.

Gallagher was also concerned over what she saw as the extravagance of staff functions that Mackay arranged for ActewAGL. Staff members from ACTEW and TransACT also attended these functions. Mackay believed that it was important to show his staff that they were valued. He thought that having functions enhanced staff morale and thereby made commercial sense. Gallagher's view was that staff members should pay to attend such functions.

She was also unhappy that Mackay, as chairman of ActewAGL, had paid $12,500 of its money at a charity auction so that he could caddy for a professional golfer in Queensland. The money went to cancer research and though Mackay paid his travel and accommodation costs, this was another occasion on which his wife's judgment was more astute than his: "I must say Colette at the time said this was a stupid thing to do."

It is impossible to know now what the outcome would have been had the error over Sullivan's salary not been made. But it is clear that Mackay had made no attempt to keep the error quiet and that there had been no intention to mislead anyone. Indeed, in all likelihood, the error would probably not have been noticed if ACTEW had not drawn it to the attention of the ACT Government bureaucracy.

What became clear to Mackay after his meeting with Gallagher was that she was quite uncomfortable with the management of ACTEW and ActewAGL and with him in particular. At the same time, the cost of the new Cotter Dam had increased from $363 million to about $410 million and ACTEW was in something of a public slanging match with the ACT Independent Competition and Regulatory Commission over the future price of Canberra's water and sewerage services.

In his defence, Mackay cited the performance of ActewAGL as by far Australia's most successful utility company. Though its retail price for electricity was among the lowest in Australia, it paid the greatest dividends to its shareholders and contributed about $2 million in sponsorship to the Canberra community. Despite this, there was something of a public and political perception that he and the organisation were extravagant.

Over the following few months, amid media accusations of attempted cover ups, excessive salaries and the apparent delay in reporting the error in an out-of-date annual report, the board of ACTEW was bombarded by letters from the Chief Minister demanding answers to numerous questions. Mackay had several meetings with the shareholders and was being worn down by the volume of correspondence and the seemingly never-ending board discussions.

From the outset he had always believed he could finagle his way out of the difficulty.

"I have always found a way of putting out a storm one way or another. I wasn't frightened to apologise or even to resign." Indeed, at his first meeting with Gallagher over this matter he asked her whether she wanted him to resign. She did not accept his resignation but neither did she beg him to stay.

Ultimately he reached the point where he decided that if he resigned it might stop the bleeding; it did. Shortly before the 15 April board meeting, in a meeting with Gallagher, he told her he believed it was time for him to go. "She was very gracious. She clearly agreed."

Although Katy Gallagher was perhaps relieved, and a little sad, she made no attempt to change his mind. But she complimented Mackay on the job he had done and left open the opportunity of his serving her government in some other capacity.

True to form, Mackay resigned on his terms. He would remain until the end of the financial year, 30 June, seeing out the completion of the dam and the final price determination by the regulator for water and sewerage services.

The day after Mackay announced his resignation, I telephoned to ask how he felt: "Fucking fantastic." It seemed that a great burden had been lifted from him. Despite his bravado, there had clearly been pain. "Underneath you are still hurting a bit, don't worry about that. I would have been hurting even if I had gone out at the absolute top of my game."

Though John was not subject to depression, even before the major row over the salary error there were days when he felt glum. "Here we are doing everything we possibly can and our shareholders are not happy. Then, after the salary thing broke, you've got this pain in your gut and I'm wondering what's this all about and how can I overcome this basic sadness."

Ensuring he was in control of the story, Mackay arranged an interview with the ABC's Adam Shirley. Mackay cycled to the studio immediately after the board meeting. "I did the interview and I really did feel a load off my shoulders as I rode back home. It was tearing the guts out of my family as well."

Soon after he announced his resignation, he and Colette went to London. As they were walking down a street he noticed that Colette was in tears. "I realised she was hurting much more than I was."

So, after ten years as CEO and five as chairman, he had few regrets that his time had come to an end. There had been many achievements and he was proud of them. "This snotty-nosed little kid from the bush had had a better run than I had ever deserved."

Fittingly, Mackay's official farewell as chairman of ACTEW and ActewAGL was held in the Village Centre at the National Arboretum on 27 June 2013.

There his good mate Allan Hawke reminded the 100 or so guests of Mackay's many achievements and contributions to Canberra—that he had been appointed a Member of the Order of Australia in June 2004 for service to the community through the management and administration of major public utility services in the ACT and for contributions to a range of health care, social welfare, cultural and sporting organisations. Hawke listed Barnados, the Smith Family, the Variety Club, Camp Quality, the Salvation Army, breast cancer charities, Canberra Cancerians, Affirm, Calvary Hospital Community Council and St John's Reid, to illustrate the breadth of organisations to which he had contributed.

"John has used his influence wherever possible, based on the philosophy that a small amount of effort can make a very big difference to community causes. It's this sustained out of hours effort and personal endeavour that distinguish his contribution."

Hawke traced Mackay's career, including his early days at ACTEW when the community became greatly concerned over the standard of its water supply. A staff member, Bob Gibbs, had rushed into Mackay's office brandishing a report and declared, "It's cryptosporidium boss!" Mackay replied, "Bob, if you think it's a good thing, have $50 each way for me."

Also paying tribute at the farewell, Katy Gallagher said she had great admiration for Mackay as a business leader. She applauded his work in the establishment of the arboretum. "You simply can't deliver a project on the scale of the arboretum without great leadership and strategic direction."

She said Mackay had advocated for the arboretum at a time when the project had been controversial and there had been many detractors. He had developed and carried the vision and taken people on the journey. "In a career of many great achievements and of such service to the Canberra community, for John this was just another day at the office."

Gallagher commended Mackay's leadership in establishing ActewAGL by integrating the disparate worlds of government and private enterprise. She acknowledged that this had founded a unique joint venture, one of the most successful businesses of its type in Australia.

"I have great admiration for how John has been a business leader with a great awareness of his influence in and his obligation to his local community." She said Mackay had established ActewAGL as a company of and for the local community. It was a major local employer and a supporter of many local causes. The company's partnership with the Centenary of Canberra showed how that culture was embedded in the organisation.

"In business as in politics, it can be the greatest adversity that shows the greatest leadership. John's role, and that of all at ActewAGL in the immediate aftermath of the 2003 fires, will mean he is always remembered as a man who stood up for Canberra in our hour of need. "Canberra was faced with 37,500 houses without power, 6,500 without gas or water, sewage treatment plants inoperable and inaccessible, and suburban communities who were on their knees. Not only did the company work around the clock in the embers of the fire to restore those essential services, it raised more than $300,000 within days to support people who had lost their homes and who had lost loved ones. Indeed, John Mackay was very much the public face of the company during that time."

Despite her flattering remarks, it must be remembered that Katy Gallagher did not seek to discourage Mackay from resigning as chairman. Yet she said, "We can all rest easy in the knowledge that in leaving ActewAGL, John will remain as a believer and a leader in this great city and will continue to make a growing contribution as we enter our second century."

She thanked him for personally supporting her, saying he had been a mentor to her as Chief Minister and to others in leadership positions.

But it was left to Allan Hawke and Mackay's successor at ActewAGL, Michael Costello, to remind the guests they were there because of the controversy over the under-reporting of Mark Sullivan's salary.

Hawke said, "I can't ignore the elephant in the room, why we are gathered here this evening. The only people who never made a mistake are those who never had a go. One of Teddy Roosevelt's quotes captures the more than fair share of ups and downs in John's life:

'It's not the critic who counts, not the one who points out how the strong man stumbled, or where the doer of good deeds might have done them better. The credit belongs to the man who is actually in the arena; whose face is marred with sweat and dust and blood; who strives valiantly; who errs and comes up short again and again; who knows the great enthusiasms, the great devotions, and spends himself in a worthy cause; who at best knows in the end the triumph of high achievement; and who at the worst, if he fails, at least fails while daring greatly, so that his place shall never be with those cold and timid souls who know neither victory nor defeat.'"

Close to tears, Costello said, "The truth is, ActewAGL is desperately sorry he is leaving, desperately sorry he is going because he's not just an A-grader, he's a state of origin player and he is a star."

Apparently genuinely, Mackay said, "I'm not the slightest bit sad tonight. I'm not angry or irritated. I'm really grateful that I got this chance and I'm really proud of what our organisations got to do along the way."

21

A FAMILY MAN AMID SUCCESS AND SETBACK

It's not hard to get John Mackay to talk about his strengths and weaknesses. But particularly after the debacle that led to his resignation as chairman of ACTEW Corporation and ActewAGL, it seemed reasonable to seek his family's perspective on the man.

John's youngest and perhaps favourite offspring, Claire, recalls that while she was at primary school, her father was often interstate or overseas. "At one point Mum figured he was gone for an average of more than three days a week for about ten years."

Despite that absence, Claire speaks about her father's profound influence on the family, particularly on her. They spent a lot of time together, and often went to Raiders Rugby League games at Canberra Stadium.

"My brother and sister [Jane and Ben] would go fishing with Dad. That was their thing they always did together."

When the family moved to O'Connor, Claire and her father could easily walk to the Stadium. From the time she was about six, they rarely missed a Raiders home game. She recalls with enthusiasm watching the Raiders win the 1994 grand final in Sydney with her parents.

After the game, John decided to go with his daughter into the Raiders' changeroom. She laughs as she recalls the experience. "For a good 75 per cent of the time we were in there, Dad had me stuck in a corner facing the wall because there were things a 12 year old girl shouldn't be seeing."

Claire was her father's favourite: "My siblings both feel I am very spoiled and I think they're probably right."

When she was a child she regarded her many adventures with her father as quite normal. As a 31 year old she recognise that they were possible only because she was the daughter of John Mackay.

There was a flight in a Tiger Moth and a ride in a hot air balloon. "He just has this way about him where interesting things happen when he is around. If it wasn't for him I wouldn't have had these opportunities."

One of their memorable adventures involved a drive to Sydney for a State of Origin Rugby League game. Claire was 15 and watched the game with her father from a corporate box. After the game, most of the other people in the box planned to bat on at a pub. John said he had to return with his daughter to their hotel. But she objected and insisted they go with the others to Kings Cross. He wasn't really convinced and even outside the pub, decided they should go to their hotel immediately, but Claire would hear nothing of it.

"I linked my arm through his and we strolled straight in through the front door of the notorious Bourbon and Beef Steak. We had this raucous night until all hours. Dad spent most of the evening guarding me in the pub, trying to make sure no young men came anywhere near me." After almost no sleep they rose early to drive back to Canberra so Claire would not be late for her part time job. Only on the highway did John notice the fuel gauge showing empty. For almost 15 kilometres they drove on fully expecting this would end badly.

"I thought 'We're going to get in trouble with Mum and I'm going to lose my job.' We managed to just coast into a petrol station with nothing in the petrol tank."

Claire still laughs about that, and about a radio interview her father did on the car phone while driving her back to school. She goaded him to phone Marty Haines on local radio station 2CC, which was raising money to buy a special piece of medical equipment to try to save a little girl, Millie, who had a rare disease.

The deal was to challenge Haines to do something funny or unusual and donate an agreed amount if he did it. Mackay dared Haines to abseil off Electricity House, but the dare backfired when Haines said he would, only if Mackay also abseiled from the 12 storey building.

The event was broadcast live as the petrified CEO and radio compere made their descent. Next day was Jane's wedding, and Betty Mackay and lots of family were watching to ensure John would be in one piece for the celebrations.

In recent years Claire has walked the Kokoda Trail, attended a kick boxing camp in Thailand, trekked in Burma and caught the notorious train from

Beijing to Moscow. She went dog sledding in Sweden with the temperature at minus 40 degrees.

Despite Claire's closeness to her family, she chose to attend boarding school in Sydney at Pymble Ladies College so she could get good marks. She used to come back to Canberra at least every second weekend, which gave her opportunities for more adventures with John. "It didn't really feel like I was that separated from life in Canberra."

Claire says both parents inculcated in all the children an amazing philosophy on life, including the family motto, "Stay Lucky". She drew from her father's example of the young boy from the bush who achieved so much. "It has kind of rubbed off on all of us kids that there is nothing which is impossible."

She went straight from school to university but did not complete the course. Her plan was to work and save some money so she could travel overseas. Instead, John offered the necessary money on the condition that when she returned she would re-enrol.

She did, but instead of continuing with a commerce-law degree she began training as a primary school teacher, with a major in management. It was later pointed out to her she would have to decide whether she was to be a primary school teacher or a business manager. So for the second time she left university without completing a degree. After working in hospitality for several years she joined the Commonwealth Public Service where she remained until mid-2013. She then headed off on an extended overseas trip, with some trepidation although she was buoyed by confidence inherited from her parents.

Claire began the journey soon after her father announced his intention to resign from the chair of ActewAGL and ACTEW. She was in awe of his ability and willingness to help people, which was a reality markedly different from the image of him portrayed in the media during the lead up to his resignation. Claire says there was a general false impression that he was someone trying to rort the system in some way.

"What I get from Dad is just how much he helps people. People do good things for Dad in return because he helps them first and it has been that way our whole life. Anyone who has ever been in a bind would come to Dad and he would open up the house. Over the time I was growing up we had so many people come to live with us during that period. People who were down on their luck or in between houses or had some bad situation. He helps people so much without thinking about it."

Despite the negative publicity, she found John remained positive while the family was distressed. The months leading to the resignation were among the most upsetting times the family had known.

Jane, the oldest of the Mackay children, studied architecture at the University of Canberra and became a successful architect. She moved with her husband Spero to the Gold Coast, where his parents lived.

Their sons, Jack and Max, were born in 2005 and 2007. They moved back to Canberra in 2009, and Jane became an architecture lecturer at the University of Canberra.

Her brother Ben moved to Queensland after leaving school. While he was working on the Sunshine Coast he learnt that he was the father of a child born in Canberra in February 1996. Although Ben contributed financially to the child's support, they would not meet for 16 years.

Ben came back to Canberra after about ten years and worked in telecommunications, initially with TransACT, then with ActewAGL.

In 2012 a young man rang John Mackay at the University of Canberra, and introduced himself as Blake Tindall. Believing him to be the son of a friend from Wellington looking for work, John asked Blake to send his CV. After their somewhat disjointed conversation, Blake sent a photograph of himself. This seemed a strange approach from someone looking for a job. While turning the matter over in his mind during opera at the Arboretum, it dawned on John that Blake was his grandson.

Next morning he phoned Ben who was delighted and arranged to meet Blake. They had breakfast, after which Ben took Blake to the Mackay house, and later on to meet Colette's parents.

Blake was wanting to become a carpenter. So John bought his grandson a utility. Blake soon found a job and has been welcomed into the family.

Colette, reflecting on 40 years of marriage, gets immediately emotional when asked to describe her husband: "Ever since I met him I have called him the light of my life because that is what he is." She wipes away tears and goes on: "He has always brought laughter into my life. I'll stop this [crying]. I am just like this."

Colette said he was still as special to her as when she sold him that raffle ticket more than 40 years ago: "He is just full of fun and laughter. When I think of John he is highly resourceful."

She remembers the time before their marriage when John worked at three jobs. She didn't see him then as ambitious: "When I first met him he was very much a Wellington boy."

She attributes much of John's resourcefulness to the freedom he had as a child: the opportunity to earn money and to have adventures with friends. "Some people are focussed on things and some people are focussed on people. He is focussed on people. In everything he does he has this instinctive, intuitive sense of what to do and how to get through things."

If she were going to a desert island and were asked what she would take with her she said the answer is: "John, because I know he would work through it. I just have this total confidence in his being able to survive in any situation whatsoever."

Colette's memory of their meeting differs from John's. She says that as part of John's work in designing forms, he had to go upstairs to the typing pool to use one of the typewriters. He would say hello, though apparently daunted by the room full of women. He would do his job and hurry out. Nevertheless, he gained enough courage to invite Colette out and she believes, the social function at Gundaroo predates the sale of the raffle ticket.

Ben provides another perspective on his father, who had an abiding interest in professional boxing. John took Ben for a boys' trip to the US and hired a legendary Chev Corvette to drive from Los Angeles to Las Vegas to see a world championship fight. The story of how John complained about a sore elbow at breakfast after a huge night out is best left on tour. We'll just say that Ben, in contrast to his father, can recall both of them riding a mechanical bull not long before dawn.

When John was courting Colette and living at Gowrie hostel in Northbourne Avenue, he made an arrangement to visit his mate Alby Sutton to watch a boxing program, TV Ringside. He neglected to mention this arrangement to Colette who was with him at Gowrie that evening. He said to her he was tired and needed to get some sleep.

Shortly after Colette walked out of the hostel, John headed for his car, only to be almost caught in Colette's headlights. He avoided discovery by hopping behind a shrub. Colette stopped to scrape ice off her windscreen, leaving the headlights pointing at the shrub behind which her future husband lurked. Then the garden sprinklers came on. John could only stay put and get soaked, and the night was not a warm one.

Eleven months after Jane's birth, Colette returned to work. About two years later she gave birth to Ben and was out of the workforce for about two years. After Claire was born in 1982, Colette was, in a way, out of the workforce for another three years. In fact, she became a child minder so she could afford to remain out of the workforce. Through Family Day Care, she minded up to six children, including Claire.

Though admiring John's resourcefulness, Colette discounts her own when she speaks without any apparent stress of catering for about 30 children and 30 adults, especially at the coast house. "John would party every single day of his life if I let him. He is constantly scheming ways of how he can have fun. Everything he does is fun. Everyone who is with him has fun."

Colette is quietly spoken but gives the impression of a certain firmness.

Who is boss in the marriage? "I think we just complement each other."

John liked her to participate in all of his social activities but there was a limit to what she was prepared to suffer. Every now and again she said that enough was enough. When he heard her say "John Mackay!" he realised he had better do as she suggested.

Life for the family, particularly for Colette, changed significantly after John joined ACTEW. For the previous 15 years or so, John had often been away from Canberra, sometimes for two or three days a week, sometimes for up to six weeks.

"It was the way the family operated and it was what we needed to do," Colette said. Though he had not spent much time with his children, especially the older two, they all idolised him.

Colette noticed the closer connection with Canberra that came with John's move to ACTEW. Life no longer revolved around the Commonwealth Public Service. She had the opportunity to attend many more functions with John involving people who ran the city of Canberra as opposed to the capital of Australia. Socially, life was "buzzing along" until about 2004. She was then working for Canberra's Land Development Agency.

But Colette became unwell and about a year later was diagnosed with breast cancer. Over the following two years she underwent surgery six times and, John says, it was a tough time. John and Colette have always been close. When she awoke from each operation he was at her bedside, and on each occasion he wept.

Shortly before one bout of surgery, they visited Beaver Gallery, where Colette saw an expensive bracelet which she suggested John might buy for her. He dismissed that suggestion by asking if she thought he was a millionaire. As she awoke from the surgery she became conscious of something on her wrist. With delight she recognised the bracelet, which John had arranged with the anaesthetist to fit after the completion of the surgery.

After Colette stopped work, she remained deeply involved in voluntary work. Her role as secretary of the Friends of the National Arboretum occupies about three days' unpaid work each week. "It is an absolutely inspirational project and it is really good to be involved with it." Though 2013 proved a tumultuous year for the Mackay family, Colette recalls earlier times when John, as a federal public servant, was exposed to public criticism. This was particularly severe when he was responsible for selling many government properties and businesses. During one six month period, The Canberra Times published about 13 column metres of material critical of John Mackay.

Still, that was nothing like the publicity that broke in early 2013 over the incorrect reporting of Mark Sullivan's salary. "We just couldn't see rhyme

Colette and John. (Picture by Lyn Mills)

nor reason for it. It was quite strange for a chief minister to come out and attack one of her own. There is no doubt that some influential people were in Katy's ear about John's largesse. Maybe he took a bullet for someone else."

Nevertheless, she was quite happy John had chosen to resign: "It enabled us as a family to move on. It affected everyone in the family."

Before his resignation, there had been many letters to the editor of *The Canberra Times* that were critical of Mackay. Colette says many letters supporting him were not published. Despite the public criticism, Colette said he was always helping someone: "He just seems to have an understanding of people and empathy with them." Again she wiped away tears.

A difference between John and Colette is their religious faith. Colette, as a committed Catholic, attends mass regularly. John respected that and said for Colette's sake he could contemplate becoming a Catholic. But Colette describes him as a true Christian. The difference between them is the name of his religion and the name of hers. "He certainly does not need to become a Catholic for my sake and I have never put that sort of pressure on him. He probably thinks more about religion at the moment because he has been working for the Catholics for about seven years."

John's role in the church organisation involves attendance at mass and tuition for about an hour on how the Catholic Church thinks about certain subjects before the beginning of each meeting of the Little Company of Mary Health Care.

For Colette, being a Catholic is part of how she lives: "It gives you an understanding and confidence in what you do. I also provide support to cancer sufferers. I think if you have religion it does help you to understand more about how to accept these things and how you deal with sickness and, well,

With daughter Jane at a University of Canberra graduation ceremony at Parliament House in 2014.

everything in your life really. You just approach things in a slightly different way."

She believes John will continue to work for many years. He is always working on something.

To a relative outsider, it seemed Colette underplayed the significance of her role in the life and career of John Mackay. When this thought is put to her she says, "I think we are a team. He does what he does really well and I do what I do pretty well and we complement each other."

But asked how he could have achieved what he has without her she admits: "He probably couldn't have."

She doesn't think the turmoil leading to his resignation brought them any closer. "I don't think it has made any difference to us. We have just come to a different part of our lives and John is picking up new things to replace the void where ActewAGL was. I think that is going really, really well."

Asked if she feels bitter about the way her husband was treated, she says she was more puzzled. "I think at the time I was upset and puzzled by it. But we have moved on and I try not to think about it now. But I still get emotional about it."

EPILOGUE
NEW VENTURES

Fallout from the error which drew so much public criticism on John Mackay and led to his resignation as chair of ACTEW Corporation and ActewAGL continued for some months after coming to the notice of ACT Chief Minister Katy Gallagher. In February, 2014, CEO Mark Sullivan departed in what was described as a "mutual decision" by him and the ACTEW board. That there was political pressure on Sullivan to leave is almost certain. Though details of his departure are covered by a contractual confidentiality clause, in its 2013/14 annual report, ACTEW recorded that Sullivan had received a termination payment of $690,000.

Later that month, ACTEW's deputy CEO, Ian Carmody, was made redundant. The annual report showed he had received $419,000 in termination payments plus $42,000 in long service leave. Then, on 20 March 2014, among other changes, acting board chair Michael Easson was confirmed as chair of the board for three years. It is fair to note that Easson had been a member of the board for at least 15 years and thus was a party to the setting of Sullivan's salary. And apparently, like other board members, he did not notice the error for which Mackay took the brunt of criticism. Yet the government made Easson chair of the board even though all who were board members at the time of the error could reasonably have been held responsible for it.

I was curious to know why a seemingly innocent error on a fairly modest scale had provoked so much ire—and belatedly triggered a barrage of condemnation which ended the ACTEW careers of John Mackay and Mark Sullivan. I made two unsuccessful requests by email to speak with Chief Minister Katy Gallagher on this matter. In both messages, I noted that the error was first recognised by the ACTEW secretary, that it was drawn to the attention of the Chief Minister and Cabinet Directorate on 9 November 2012, and that the directorate did not notify the Chief Minister until March 2013.

So, was it the amount Sullivan was being paid, with ACTEW board approval, which upset the Chief Minister, or was it the error in the 2010/11 annual report? That question remains unanswered.

Despite the row over Sullivan's annual salary, his replacement, John Knox, was engaged in March 2014 on an annual salary of $693,000—the same as Sullivan's termination payout.

Over a year after Mackay's departure from ACTEW Corporation and ActewAGL, scars remain. He might contest this, but to a relatively independent observer, it seemed that he carried some emotional hurt from the row that followed the discovery of the error in the annual report.

But it would be a serious error to suggest the row and his subsequent resignation had diminished his enthusiasm for life, for fun, comradeship and the opportunity to serve others on numerous boards. Though he might reflect on what he saw as the unfairness of 2013, he was not a changed man. He simply redirected some of his considerable energy to other ventures.

His optimism, enthusiasm and ebullient nature remain undented. So too his commitment to Canberra and its residents. He came to know and to serve Canberrans while responsible for overseeing the supply of electricity, gas, water and the construction of a broadband network. The everyday people John Mackay came to know are not reflected in daily news reports from Canberra to the rest of Australia. They are the people who make up a community largely separate from national politics.

When he was not travelling for business or pleasure—sometimes the line between them was indistinct—John enjoyed Canberra for its restaurants, golf courses and mates. Then there is his other love—the coast house at Mossy Point. There he has time and space for reflection and entertaining, though probably not both at once.

Despite the trauma of 2013, life went on at a similar pace. It could not reasonably be described as retirement, but there is greater freedom to direct energy to causes which take his fancy. He is on the boards of the University of Canberra, Little Company of Mary Healthcare Australia, CIC Australia, SpeedCast (Hong Kong), National Arboretum Canberra, DataPod Australia, and his beloved Canberra Raiders. John is taking a leading role in building a respite centre for children with autism, on behalf of the Ricky Stuart Foundation, and has already secured the land, an architect and a project manager.

At the time of writing he was preparing for board meetings in London and Rotterdam, and planning another barging adventure in France. With all of these interests, John Mackay might not live quite as much on the edge as previously, but that edge has never been too far away.

KEY DATES

1950   Born in Wellington, New South Wales

1957–67 Top Cub Scout, Scout and cadet

1968   Obtained a pass in six subjects in the Higher School Certificate at Wellington High School; bulldozer driver, "Auscott," Warren, New South Wales

1969   Moved to Canberra and joined the Department of Immigration as base-grade clerk

1972   Married Colette Carmody; joined the Department of Primary Industry as Forms Officer (Class 5)

1973   First child Jane born

1975   Joined the Department of the Prime Minister and Cabinet as an Internal Consultant (Class 7), later became Chief Personnel Officer; began part-time study at Canberra College of Advanced Education (later the University of Canberra); second child Ben born

1979   Father Jack died in Wellington, aged 74; full-time student on a Free Place scholarship to complete a degree majoring in administration and economics; joined the Public Service Board as a recruitment policy and administration officer (Class 9)

1980   Graduated with prize as top student in final year of Administrative Studies

1981   Promoted to the Department of Housing and Construction as a Personnel Policy and Industrial Relations senior manager (Class 10)

1982   Third child Claire born

1987   Moved to the Department of Administrative Services as an industrial relations junior executive

1989   Appointed as Senior Private Secretary to the Hon. Stuart West, Federal Minister for Administrative Services; brothers David and Stephen died of AIDS

1990   Appointed General Manager, Overseas Property Group

1991   Appointed Director, Australian Protective Service

1994   Appointed Deputy Secretary (Commercial), Department of Administrative Services

1998   Appointed CEO of ACT Electricity and Water Corporation (ACTEW);

2000   Appointed CEO of the ActewAGL joint venture; appointed a Director of TransACT Communications; daughter Jane married Spero Cassidy

2004   Appointed a Member (AM) of the Order of Australia

2005   Wife Colette diagnosed with breast cancer

2006   Ran a leg of the Commonwealth Games torch relay

2007   Mother Betty died in Dubbo Base Hospital, aged 89

2008   Resigned as CEO of ActewAGL and appointed as Chairman of ACTEW Corporation, ActewAGL joint venture and TransACT Communications Pty Ltd; Koomarri's Belconnen building named The John Mackay Centre by the Prime Minister's wife, Thérèse Rein; ran a leg of the Beijing Olympic torch relay

2009   Appointed Canberra Citizen of the Year

2010   Awarded Honorary Doctorate by the University of Canberra

2011   Inducted as Chancellor of the University of Canberra

2012   Awarded Grande Order of Bernardo O'Higgins by the President of Chile

2013   Resigned as Chair of ACTEW Corporation and ActewAGL joint venture

2014   Current roles: Chairman, Speedcast (Hong Kong); Council member, the University of Canberra; directorships: Little Company of Mary Healthcare, CIC Australia, Datapod Australia, Canberra Raiders, Ricky Stuart Foundation.

Retirement function at the National Arboretum, with some influential "scaly mates": Mikael Svensson (Hyatt), former department secretaries Jeff Harmer AO and Allan Hawke AC, executive recruiter Ian Hansen, Brian Acworth AM (Westpac), US ambassador Jeff Bleich, Dr Peter Yorke, Allan Williams (Qantas) and Paul Walshe (ActewAGL marketing executive). (Picture by Lyn Mills)

INDEX OF NAMES